LUTHER and BACH on the MAGNIFICAT

LUTHER and BACH on the MAGNIFICAT

For Advent and Christmas

PETER A. HENDRICKSON
BRADLEY C. JENSON
RANDI H. LUNDELL

With a Foreword by Hans H. Wiersma

WIPF & STOCK · Eugene, Oregon

LUTHER AND BACH ON THE MAGNIFICAT
For Advent and Christmas

Copyright © 2015 Peter A. Hendrickson, Bradley C. Jenson, and Randi H. Lundell. All rights reserved. Except for brief quotations in critical publications or reviews, no part of this book may be reproduced in any manner without prior written permission from the publisher. Write: Permissions, Wipf and Stock Publishers, 199 W. 8th Ave., Suite 3, Eugene, OR 97401.

Scripture quotations taken from the New Revised Standard Version Bible, copyright 1989, Division of Christian Education of the National Council of Churches of Christ in the United States of America. Used by permission. All rights reserved.

Wipf & Stock
An imprint of Wipf and Stock Publishers
199 W. 8th Ave., Suite 3
Eugene, OR 97401

www.wipfandstock.com

ISBN 13: 978-1-62564-120-5

Manufactured in the U.S.A.   09/09/2015

To the late Bradford Tracey
(Peter Hendrickson's harpsichord teacher in Berlin)

To Jill Jenson
(Bradley Jenson's wife)

To Roy and Norma Harrisville
(Randi Lundell's parents)

Contents

Acknowledgments | ix
Foreword by Hans H. Wiersma | xi
Preface | xiii

1 Introduction to Luther's *Commentary on the Magnificat* | 1
2 Introduction to Bach's *Magnificat* | 13
3 Luther's *Commentary on the Magnificat* | 21
   THE MAGNIFICAT
4 Bach on the Magnificat | 80
5 Luther and Lutheranism on Mary in an Ecumenical Context | 100

Appendix: Using This Book in a Group Setting | 113

Bibliography | 117
About the Contributors | 119

Acknowledgments

THE CONTRIBUTORS TO THIS book wish to thank Dr. Jill D. Jenson of the University of Minnesota Duluth for the untold hours she spent reading, editing, and commenting on this book. Working with several writers on one project is challenging, but her skills with the written word brought focus, clarity, and consistency to the entire text. Of course, any errors that might remain are our responsibility. We also thank Dr. Joseph A. Burgess, a former participant in and coeditor of the US Lutheran–Roman Catholic dialogues, for his helpful editorial suggestions. Before work on this book actually began, the concept for it was used in a three-week "Word and Music" Advent study event offered through New Life Lutheran Church in Duluth, Minnesota, beginning in 2012. The book took shape as those studies continued during the Advent seasons of 2013 and 2014. We thank New Life Lutheran's pastor, the Rev. David S. Norland, for his excellent teaching on the *Magnificat*, and also the participants in the study over the past three years for their enthusiasm, diligence, and helpful suggestions. Finally, we thank Dr. Hans H. Wiersma for writing the foreword to this book.

—Peter A. Hendrickson, Bradley C. Jenson, and Randi H. Lundell

I would like to thank, *in memoriam*, Bradford Tracey, professor of harpsichord at the Hochschule der Künste in West Berlin, for opening the door to Baroque music for me. I also want to thank, *in memoriam*, my uncle Matt Mattson, who suggested that I build a harpsichord when I was fifteen years old. My thanks go to Paul Boehnke, artistic director of the Bach Society of Minnesota, for his insights into the musical language of Bach. Finally, thanks to my wife, Mindy Keskinen, for her tremendous support.

—Peter A. Hendrickson

Foreword

AT THE START OF this volume, it's important to remember what all the fuss is about: namely, a surprise pregnancy announced two millennia ago. That's a blunt introduction, but there it is. No matter the genius and complexity evident in Luther's commentary or in Bach's composition, at the heart of the Magnificat is, of course, the Incarnation of the Creator inside of the creation—inside of one of his creatures. A young woman's womb is, one would think, no place for the Maker of the heavens and of the earth but, again, there it is.

Mary's hymn recorded at the end of the first chapter of Luke represents a teenager's inspired attempt to set the ineffable to words and music. Luther's creative exposition of Mary's exclamation and Bach's imaginative rendering of Mary's tune further magnify Mary's magnification of what God has done. In the face of impossible news—the announcement of the Divine taking human flesh—the Bible gives us Mary's voice magnifying her Lord. And that would have been good enough. However, along the way, the good Lord has seen fit to inspire a wealth of exegesis and music inspired by the Magnificat. Over the centuries, such helpful resources have guided believers to better understand and appreciate Mary's song. Historically speaking, Luther's commentary and Bach's composition are among the best known of these resources. And now you hold in your hands a resource that will aid you in better understanding Luther's and Bach's understanding of Mary's psalm of praise.

Luther and Bach on the Magnificat represents the collective erudition and expertise of three respected scholars. These three are here united under a single cover to bring you the definitive word on Luther's and Bach's works with Mary's psalm. Consider the depth and breadth of the scholarship contained herein. First, at the heart of the volume, is Randi Lundell's accessible and readable translation of Luther's commentary. Her work represents a

Foreword

fine English language update—the first since the Steinhaeuser translation over one hundred years ago. Surrounding Luther's commentary, as well as Bach's composition, are the incisive theological, biblical, confessional, historical, and musical illuminations engagingly crafted by Luther scholar Brad Jenson and Bach scholar Peter Hendrickson.

As will be made plain further on, this volume is best digested as part of a broader activity. The authors rightly recommend concurrent and collective engagement with Luther's commentary and Bach's composition. In other words, get a CD or DVD of Bach's *Magnificat*, listen in the company of others, and use this book to help you "hear" all that Mary sings. (Several recommended recordings are suggested in the pages ahead.) Since Bach composed his take on the *Magnificat* during the Advent season and first presented it on Christmas Day, it makes sense to use this book beginning in the season of Advent (as the authors recommend). However, since Bach's *Magnificat* also represents a sung version of the kind of *theologia crucis* (theology of the cross) propounded by Luther, *Luther and Bach on the Magnificat* could also lend a compelling subtext during the season of Lent (although during Lent you'd want to skip the Lauds).

In any case, no matter the time or season, this volume should inspire you to experience the Magnificat in such a way that you might find yourself joining your voice to Mary's and singing, "My soul magnifies the Lord!"

—Hans H. Wiersma
Augsburg College

Preface

THIS BOOK HAD ITS beginnings in the late 1980s, when I was searching for a contemporary advent devotional that reflected Martin Luther's theology. I found none better than Luther's *Commentary on the Magnificat* (Mary's hymn of praise in the Gospel of Luke 1:46–55). I have used it as my Advent devotional ever since. Luther's commentary was not written specifically for Advent/Christmas, but it is an excellent text for the season. It is indeed a spiritual classic, and as such it has been and always will be "contemporary."

A few years ago, I realized that the text of the Magnificat afforded a unique opportunity to bring together the gifts of Lutheranism's original and most prominent theologian with Lutheranism's most prominent composer/musician, Johann Sebastian Bach. Martin Luther wrote his *Commentary on the Magnificat* in 1521, more than two hundred years before Bach composed his *Magnificat* in E-flat major for Christmas in 1723. Bach clearly had Luther on his mind as he composed his cantata because he incorporated a Christmas hymn written by Luther into his musical masterpiece. It was in recognizing and thinking about this connection between Luther and Bach on the Magnificat that the idea for this book was born. The timing for such a book seemed ideal. We are just a few years away from the five-hundredth anniversary of the Lutheran Reformation, which will likely result in a growing interest in all things by and about Martin Luther. At the same time, there will hopefully be a revival of interest in Bach's deep roots in Lutheran theology.

How did this project come together? Originally I planned on writing the introduction to Luther's commentary and a chapter on Luther and Lutheranism on Mary, but a team would be required to make *Luther and Bach on the Magnificat* a reality. A fresh translation of Luther's *Commentary on the Magnificat* from German to English was necessary. My connection with Dr. Randi Lundell was through my seminary advisor, Dr. Roy A. Harrisville, who is Dr. Lundell's father. After making contact with Randi, I became

Preface

impressed by the number of theological works she had translated from German to English. I was delighted when she agreed to work on this book and provide a fresh translation of Luther's commentary. It was Randi who suggested that I contact Dr. Peter Hendrickson about writing the sections on Bach, which he happily agreed to do. He is Director of Choral Activities at Augsburg College in Minneapolis, where he conducts the Augsburg Choir and the Masterworks Chorale of Augsburg. As Artistic Director of the Masterworks Chorale of Augsburg, Peter conducted a performance of Bach's *Magnificat* in 2009.

The result of the collaboration is this book—written for a general audience—that can be used as an Advent/Christmas devotional study by individuals or in group settings in congregations. Of course, to get the most out of what this book offers, readers need to secure a recording of a performance of Bach's *Magnificat* from a local music store or an online retailer. While there are a number of recordings currently available, here are some suggestions:

- In DVD format, there is an excellent performance of Bach's *Magnificat* in E-flat major by the Amsterdam Baroque Orchestra and Choir, Ton Koopman conducting, performed at the 2003 Bachfest Leipzig in the Church of St. Thomas, where Bach was once the cantor (music director).

- In CD format, there are two recordings in E-flat major. One is titled *J. S. Bach Magnificat: A Bach Christmas*, by the New London Consort, Philip Picket conducting. The other is *J. S. Bach Leipziger Weihnachtskantaten: Cantates de Noël à Leipzig* (*Christmas Cantatas from Leipzig*), by the Collegium Vocale Gent, Philippe Herreweghe conducting. Recordings in E-flat major are rare because Bach's transposition of his *Magnificat* into D major became more popular than his original E-flat major composition. However, the E-flat major version includes the Lauds (Christmas interpolations), so it is preferred for the Christmas season. In addition to the *Magnificat*, both of these CDs include recordings of other Bach Christmas cantatas, such as *Christen, ätzet diesen Tag* (Christian, Etch This Day, BWV[1] 63), which Bach also directed on Christmas Day of 1723 in Leipzig. Yes, two powerful

---

1. BWV stands for Bach-Werke-Verzeichnis (German), which translated means "Bach's Works Catalogue" and is the numbering system for referencing Bach's compositions.

Preface

cantatas, composed and directed by Bach, were presented at the *same* Christmas celebration!

- As mentioned above, there are a number of recordings of Bach's *Magnificat* available in D major, but they do not include the Lauds that are included in Bach's original E-flat major composition. In D major, the Phillips Digital Classics recording by the Monteverdi Choir, John Eliot Gardiner conducting, is recommended.

This book is organized with an introduction to Luther's *Commentary on the Magnificat* in chapter 1 followed by an introduction to Bach's *Magnificat* in chapter 2. Chapter 3 presents Dr. Lundell's new translation of Luther's commentary. Chapter 4 offers a brief summary of Luther's comments on each particular verse of Luke's text (Luke 1:46–55) that corresponds to movements in Bach's *Magnificat*, followed by helpful information on how to understand Bach's musical composition. Chapter 5 provides an overview of how Luther and Lutheranism understand the Virgin Mary in a wider ecumenical context. Finally, the Appendix offers suggestions for using this book in a congregational or other group setting.

In order to get the most out of this book for spiritual edification during the Advent/Christmas season, it is helpful to *study* Luther's commentary rather than just read it. In other words, read it and reread it during the Advent/Christmas season. At the same time, it is helpful to listen to a recording of Bach's *Magnificat* many times during the season. You will soon be caught up in the beauty of the Latin words set to Bach's music as they interpret the significance of the Magnificat. The translation from Latin to English in chapter 2 or chapter 4 will guide you as you listen to the performance.

In Martin Luther's time, the Magnificat was sung at Vespers (evening prayers) on a daily basis. Of course, that is not the case today in most churches, but if you become immersed in the Magnificat during the Advent/Christmas season every year, you will find that doing so is an excellent Word-and-music study and devotional experience. In this spirit, I sincerely hope that this year and each year going forward your Advent and Christmas seasons are blessed by your reading of Luther's spiritual classic and your listening to Bach's musical masterpiece, as Luther and Bach interpret the Virgin Mary's singularly beautiful hymn of praise to God.

Soli Deo Gloria,

—Rev. Bradley C. Jenson
Duluth, Minnesota
Advent 2014

1

Introduction to Luther's *Commentary on the Magnificat*

THE VIRGIN MARY'S STORY in the Gospel according to Luke begins with the amazing Annunciation, the angel Gabriel's announcement to Mary that she will miraculously conceive a son, Jesus, the Son of God (Luke 1:26–38). The angel also told Mary that Elizabeth, a relative of hers who was beyond child-bearing years, had conceived a son: "For nothing will be impossible with God" (1:37).

After the angel departed from Mary, she journeyed to a Judean town to see Elizabeth. This story, known as the Visitation, is where we find the Magnificat, Mary's song of praise to God. The name Magnificat comes from the Latin verb *magnifico*, which means to magnify, praise, or glorify. This is the first word in the Latin version of Mary's song: *Magnificat anima mea Dominum*, "My soul magnifies the Lord" (1:46).

The full text of this beautiful expression of Mary's glorification of God appears below in English from the New Revised Standard Version Bible:

> The Magnificat: Luke 1:46–55
>
> 46 And Mary said,
>   "My soul magnifies the Lord,
> 47 and my spirit rejoices in God
>   my Savior,
> 48 for he has looked with favor on the
>   lowliness of his servant.
>   Surely, from now on all generations

will call me blessed;
49 for the Mighty One has done great
    things for me,
  and holy is his name.
50 His mercy is for those who fear him
  from generation to generation.
51 He has shown strength with his arm;
  he has scattered the proud in the
    thoughts of their hearts.
52 He has brought down the powerful
    from their thrones,
  and lifted up the lowly;
53 he has filled the hungry with
    good things,
  and sent the rich away empty.
54 He has helped his servant Israel,
  in remembrance of his mercy,
55 according to the promise he made to
    our ancestors,
  to Abraham and to his descendants forever."

What follows is both a historical and a theological introduction to Martin Luther's *Commentary on the Magnificat*.

HISTORICAL INTRODUCTION

Martin Luther began writing his *Commentary on the Magnificat*, the book that interprets Mary's song of praise, toward the end of 1520. This was a very significant year for Luther because on June 24, 1520, the pope published a bull (i.e., an official papal document) threatening to excommunicate Luther if he did not recant his Reformation teaching. The bull, however, did not reach Luther at Wittenberg until October 10, 1520. He was given sixty days from the date of receipt to recant, which, of course, Luther refused to do. Precisely sixty days after the papal bull reached Wittenberg, Luther publicly burned it along with the Roman Catholic canon law (official church law). The die was cast. On January 3, 1521, Rome issued the final bull of excommunication against Luther and his followers. Luther was now formally considered a heretic, and he knew what happened one hundred years earlier to the reformer John Hus after he was excommunicated: Hus was burned at the stake. Although execution did not automatically follow a bull of excommunication, Luther knew he was in a very difficult situation and

Introduction to Luther's *Commentary on the Magnificat*

that his safety was in jeopardy. This was the situation Luther faced when he began work on his *Commentary on the Magnificat*.

With respect to his personal safety, Luther remained under the protection of his German prince, Elector Frederick the Wise of Saxony. Whereas Frederick was cautious to not openly support Luther, his young nephew Prince John Frederick did. Out of gratitude for the young prince's public support, Luther wrote and dedicated his *Commentary* to John Frederick.

In the winter of 1521, Luther was focused on finishing the *Commentary*, but he was summoned to appear before Emperor Charles V at the Imperial Diet (an assembly of German princes, a number of prince-bishops, and other rulers), which was held at Worms, Germany. The crisis was deepening for Luther. He interrupted his writing to prepare to defend his teaching at Worms. On March 10, 1521, Luther wrote his letter of dedication to Prince John Frederick even though the *Commentary* itself was unfinished. On March 31, 1521, just a couple of days prior to his leaving for Worms, Luther sent the letter of dedication and the partially finished manuscript to John Frederick. The rest of the manuscript would have to wait until after the proceedings at the Imperial Diet.

On April 17, 1521, Luther appeared before the emperor at the Imperial Diet. Luther was asked directly to state whether or not he would recant his books and his teachings. In response, Luther gave his famous "Here I Stand" speech, which became one of the most significant historical moments in European history as well as in the history of the entire Christian Church. Luther said:

> Unless I am convinced by the testimony of the Scriptures or by clear reason (for I do not trust either in the pope or the councils alone, since it is well known that they have often erred and contradicted themselves), I am bound by the Scriptures I have quoted and my conscience is captive to the Word of God. I cannot and I will not retract anything, since it is neither safe nor right to go against conscience. May God help me. Amen.[1]

Prince John Frederick's uncle, Elector Frederick the Wise, was present when Luther gave his speech and he shared his thoughts about Luther's speech with his court chaplain, George Spalatin: "'Father Martinus spoke well before the Lord Emperor, all the princes, and the estates.' But, the cautious Elector also added, 'He is much too bold for me.'"[2]

---

1. Brecht, *Martin Luther*, 460.
2. Ibid., 461–62.

In this judicial proceeding concerning Luther, the emperor had promised Luther safe passage both to and from the assembly at Worms, but after that journey Luther's life would likely be in danger. For this reason, on the night of May 3, 1521, on Luther's way back to Wittenberg, a small number of his supporters staged a fake kidnapping. They whisked him off to the Wartburg Castle, where he remained in hiding under the alias "Knight George." As theologian James Kittelson wrote, "It was all so well done that even the elector [Frederick the Wise] could honestly report that he did not know Luther's whereabouts."[3]

On May 25, 1521, Emperor Charles V issued the Edict of Worms, which officially put Luther under the imperial ban. Now Luther was both a heretic and an outlaw. The imperial ban meant that Luther had now formally been given a death sentence.

Nevertheless, from the safety of Wartburg Castle in Saxony, Luther resumed his writing. His most immediate concern was to finish his *Commentary on the Magnificat* for Prince John Frederick. On June 10, 1521, Luther sent the completed manuscript to the Saxon court chaplain, George Spalatin, for printing. By August, Luther had grown increasingly anxious that the *Magnificat* still had not been published, and he wrote to his friend and colleague Philip Melanchthon on August 3, 1521: "'I am amazed that my Magnificat is not finished yet. . . . Who knows whether this may not be the end of my ministry? . . . Yet I have not lived in vain.' A few days later, on August 6, 1521, he wrote to Spalatin: 'I implore you, is my Magnificat finished yet?'"[4] There is evidence that the manuscript was finally in print by September 6, 1521. According to theologian Jaroslav Pelikan, "The commentary seems to have achieved rather wide distribution; the Weimar edition [of Luther's Works] lists eight separate printings in the next five years, in addition to two printings of a Latin translation."[5]

Luther's *Commentary on the Magnificat* was first translated into English by Albert T. W. Steinhaeuser in the early 1900s and was included in the Philadelphia or Holman edition of *Luther's Works*. A revised version of the Steinhaeuser translation is included in volume 21 of the American Edition of *Luther's Works*. In 1956, Concordia Publishing House made Luther's *Commentary on the Magnificat* more accessible to the general public by publishing it as a stand-alone book. In 1967, the 450th anniversary of

---

3. Kittelson, *Luther the Reformer*, 163.
4. Luther, *Luther's Works* (hereafter *LW*), vol. 21, xviii–xix.
5. Ibid., xix.

Introduction to Luther's *Commentary on the Magnificat*

the Lutheran Reformation, Augsburg Publishing House offered a paperback edition of Luther's *Commentary* with a brief introduction by church historian E. Clifford Nelson. The new translation of Luther's *Commentary* by Randi Lundell provided here in this present book is the first English translation published since the Steinhaeuser translation was completed over one hundred years ago. The timing of this new translation is especially appropriate as we approach the 500th anniversary of the Lutheran Reformation in 2017 and the 500th anniversary of the original publication Luther's *Commentary on the Magnificat* in 2021.

THEOLOGICAL INTRODUCTION

The cross alone is our theology. —Martin Luther

As mentioned above, in 1967 Augsburg Publishing House published Luther's *Commentary on the Magnificat* in paperback. In E. Clifford Nelson's introduction to the *Commentary*, he wrote that Luther delighted in the Magnificat as "a magnificent witness to what he had already (1518) called *theologia crucis* [the theology of the cross]...."[6] Indeed, Luther's *Commentary on the Magnificat* is an exposition of his theology of the cross in the form of a doxology, a hymn of praise to God. In order to better understand the connection between Luther's theology of the cross and the Magnificat as a doxology, it is helpful to define Luther's theology of the cross and then explore how his theology finds expression through what is known as the Reformation *solas*, the "alones": Christ *alone*, cross *alone*, faith *alone*, Word *alone*, Scripture *alone*, grace *alone*, and to the glory of God *alone*.[7]

What is Martin Luther's theology of the cross? It might help to begin by saying what the theology of the cross is *not*. The theology of the cross is not a narrowing of the Bible's message to the events that happened on Good Friday. Rather, the theology of the cross is a perspective from which to view all of the important events of the New Testament. Regarding Luther's theology of the cross, theologian Herman Sasse wrote that the major New Testament events—Christmas, Easter, and Pentecost—cannot be understood without the connection to Good Friday. For Luther, the manger scene, the empty tomb, and the event of Pentecost all stand in the shadow

---

6. Luther, *Commentary on the Magnificat*, trans. Steinhaeuser, 7–8.

7. For a discussion about how the Reformation *solas* work together, see *The Cross and the Crown* by the CrossAlone District of LCMC.

of the cross of Christ and cannot be properly understood apart from the cross.[8] Furthermore, as theologian Gerhard Forde has written, Luther's theology of the cross is deeply rooted in the Old Testament as well. As such, Luther's theology of the cross does not narrow the biblical message to focus exclusively on the crucifixion, but, rather, everything else in Scripture finds its true significance *in relation to* the crucifixion of Christ. It is in this broad sense that Luther could say, "The cross alone is our theology."

The theology of the cross is a preaching theology. As such, its aim is the proclamation of the Word of God as law and Gospel. When the theology of the cross is proclaimed, the first thing it does is to attack sin. Of course, other theologies attack sin too. What is unique about the theology of the cross is that it is more than an attack on human vices. It is also, and primarily, an attack on human and religious *virtues*, an attack on *good works*, as Gerhard Forde made clear:

> The cross is in the first instance God's attack on human sin. Of course in the second instance, and finally, it is also salvation from sin. . . . As an attack it reveals that the real seat of sin is not in the flesh but in our *spiritual* aspirations. . . . Therefore the theology of the cross is an offensive theology. The offense consists in the fact that unlike other theologies it attacks what we usually consider the best in our religion. As we shall see, theologians of the cross do not worry so much about what is obviously bad in our religion, our bad works, as they do about pretension that comes with our good works.[9]

Why attack virtues and good works? How can they be sinful? How can the "real seat of sin" be "spiritual aspirations"? Virtues, good works, and other such spiritual aspirations are "the real seat of sin" because they are the means by which people attempt to justify themselves before God. They are the means of human works-righteousness. In preaching, these forms of works-righteousness are to be nullified so that the hearers of the Word of God can then be justified by faith *alone* as a free gift from God. For only by being justified by faith *alone* can a person give all the glory to God *alone* rather than reserving glory for him- or herself. This is why the theology of the cross attacks "what we usually consider best in our religion."

Therefore, we would expect this attack to find expression in Luther's *Commentary on the Magnificat*. We would expect to find Luther writing in

---

8. Sasse, *We Confess Jesus Christ*, 39.
9. Forde, *On Being a Theologian of the Cross*, 1–2.

Introduction to Luther's *Commentary on the Magnificat*

terms of the theology of the cross by specifying God's attack on what is best in human and religious virtue. Early in the *Commentary*, Luther does just that: "[God] makes everything that was valuable, honorable, holy, and alive into nothing; into something small, despised, paltry, and dead."[10] What is considered "valuable, honorable, holy, and alive" would be what is normally considered to be best in one's religion, but these attributes are under attack by the Word of God. It is precisely when the Reformation *solas* are preached that they perform this vital function of attacking what, in pious terms, is honorable and virtuous.

Indeed, when preached, the *solas* function in such a way that the hearers become, in the Apostle Paul's words, "crucified with Christ." Therefore Paul, in writing about justification by faith alone apart from the works of the law, says of himself, "For through the law I died to the law, so that I might live to God. I have been crucified with Christ; and it is no longer I who live, but it is Christ who lives in me. And the life I now live in the flesh I live by faith in the Son of God, who loved me and gave himself up for me" (Galatians 2:19–20). Thus it is through the preaching of the "alones" that the pious person is crucified and dies to the law. When people are completely cut off from their virtues and good works, they become "small, despised, paltry, and dead"—they become crucified with Christ in order to be raised up through the Gospel to "live by faith in the Son of God." This is how the theology of the cross is a preaching theology.

For the sake of further clarity, it is helpful to contrast the theology of the cross with theologies of glory—which all other theologies are. Gerhard Forde wrote, "Theologians of glory operate with fundamentally different presuppositions about how one comes to know God. . . . [For any theology of glory to work] there must be a 'glory road,' a way of law, which the fallen creature can traverse by willing and working and thus gain the necessary merit eventually to arrive at glory."[11] In other words, under all theologies of glory a person must *do something* in order to receive God's gift of salvation. For the theology of the cross, there is no "glory road" at all. There is no way for the fallen human being to fulfill the requirements of God's law. There is no *something that can be done* by a person to receive salvation. Salvation is all God's doing.

Therefore, for Luther the Magnificat is a true *Soli Deo gloria* (To God alone be the glory). Moreover, it is Mary's *Soli Deo gloria*. The vital key to

---

10. See page 25.
11. Forde, *On Being a Theologian of the Cross*, 12.

interpreting the Magnificat is found in the word "alone." "To God alone be the glory" means that none of the glory is reserved for the pious pilgrim on a glory road and none is reserved even for Mary herself. To God alone be the glory means precisely that: the glory is God's alone. Why? Because the event of salvation, beginning with the Incarnation of which Mary sings, is accomplished by God's grace alone. Therefore, the great New Testament story of the miraculous conception and birth of Jesus Christ—which certainly involves Mary—is all to the glory of God. This is why the theology of the cross goes hand-in-glove with *Soli Deo gloria*.

The Cross and the Crown, a book on the Reformation *solas*, points out that, historically speaking, *Soli Deo gloria* has not been one of the "Lutheran distinctives" in the same formulaic way as has Christ *alone*, cross *alone*, faith *alone*, Word *alone*, Scripture *alone*, and grace *alone*.[12] The section on "To God Alone the Glory" in *The Cross and the Crown* ends with this quote from Luther:

> Luther on giving all the glory to God: "When my movement first began, Dr. Staupitz, a very worthy man and the vicar of the Augustinian Order, said to me: 'It pleases me very much that this doctrine of ours gives glory and everything else solely to God and nothing at all to men; for it is as clear as day that it is impossible to ascribe too much glory, goodness, etc., to God.' So it was that he consoled me. And it is true that the doctrine of the Gospel takes away all glory, wisdom, righteousness, etc., from men and gives it solely to the Creator, who makes all things out of nothing. Furthermore, it is far safer to ascribe too much to God than to men."[LW 26:66][13]

For Luther, then, the Magnificat is the Virgin Mary proclaiming a song of witness to the theology of the cross as a doxology: *Soli Deo gloria*.

Luther's Theological Understanding of Mary in His Commentary on the Magnificat

Luther's portrait of Mary in his *Commentary* "is the embodiment of God's unmerited grace."[14] In keeping with the Old Testament prophecy, Mary "is of the royal stem and line of David,"[15] but that is not to be interpreted as her

---

12. CrossAlone District, *Cross and the Crown*, 52.
13. Ibid., 56.
14. Anderson et al., eds., *One Mediator*, 236.
15. See page 27.

Introduction to Luther's *Commentary on the Magnificat*

merit for being chosen to bear the Christ Child. As one who receives God's unmerited grace, Mary declares, "My soul magnifies the Lord." She gives God the glory for what he has done for her rather than magnifying herself for being chosen to give birth to the Son of God. With respect to her great blessing, Luther wrote that "the glory all goes to God who alone deserves it."[16] Thus Mary's witness to being chosen to be the Mother of God is a powerful *Soli Deo gloria*! With respect to Mary herself, Luther developed three themes based on Mary's hymn of praise. First, Luther highlighted Mary's lowly state as a maid in Nazareth. Second, Luther focused on Mary as the Mother of God. Third, Luther interpreted Mary's teaching about the work of God.

Mary's Lowly State as a Maid in Nazareth

First, Luther expounded on what Mary means by acknowledging her lowly state in life. He does so by comparing and contrasting Mary's lowly situation with other women of higher situation in life:

> Mary's meaning here [in Luke 1:48] is: "God has regarded me, a poor, despised, lowly girl, though he could have found a rich, famous, noble, mighty queen, or the daughter of a prince or lord. He could have found the daughter of Annas or of Caiaphas, men who held the highest position in the land, but instead he cast his pure and gracious eyes on me and used a lowly, despised maiden so that no one would boast that they were worthy of it. And I must acknowledge that this is all due to pure grace and goodness and not my own merit or worthiness."[17]

But Mary's lowly state is not singled out for praise. Instead, God is to be praised for *regarding her* in her lowly state. God, in his grace and glory, looked upon Mary and chose her for the great honor of giving birth to the Son of God.

Mary as the Mother of God

Second, Luther focused on Mary as the Mother of God. When Mary sang that God "has done great things" for her, this refers to her being chosen to

---

16. See page 33.
17. See page 38.

become the Mother of God. Luther commented that "so many great and good things were given to her that they are beyond human understanding. For from this flows all honor and blessing and her peerless place among all humankind, since there is no one like her, because she had a child by our heavenly Father...."[18] Therefore, Mary sang her *Soli Deo gloria* in Luke 1:46–49 both in reference to God's goodness and grace in regarding her in her lowly estate and in choosing her to be the human mother who would give birth to the one who is God.

Mary as Teacher of the Works of God

Third, Luther interpreted Mary's teaching about the works of God in the final six verses of the Magnificat. Luther wrote, "Now that she has sung about herself and God's goodness to her and has sung God's praises, Mary walks us through the works that God does for all people and praises them, teaching us to understand the works, ways, nature, and will of God."[19] Mary summarizes six works of God: (1) granting mercy, (2) destroying spiritual pride, (3) bringing down the powerful, (4) exhalting the lowly, (5) filling the hungry with good things, and (6) sending the rich away empty.

For Prince John Frederick, as a future ruler, Luther considered the first two of Mary's teachings most important: God's granting mercy and his destroying spiritual pride. In the epilogue to his *Commentary*, Luther addressed the prince directly:

> I also ask and mildly recommend to Your Serene Highness that for all of your days you will fear nothing more on the earth—even in hell—than what the Mother of God here calls the "disposition of one's heart." For that is the greatest, closest, mightiest, most pernicious enemy of all people and primarily of overlords; namely, reason, good intentions or discretion, from which all advice and regimes must draw. And Your Serene Highness cannot be safe from it if you do not always challenge prudence and follow in the fear of God.[20]

It may seem strange that Luther selected what people might think is the best that a ruler could have—reason, good intentions, or discretion—and declared that together they are "the most pernicious enemy of all people

---

18. See page 49–50.
19. See page 54.
20. See page 78.

Introduction to Luther's *Commentary on the Magnificat*

and primarily of overlords...."[21] One would think that a prince who ruled with reason, good intentions, and discretion would be considered a good and wise ruler. But Luther is telling the prince it is precisely these good and virtuous qualities that can lead to spiritual pride. Spiritual pride, in turn, leads to a prince's downfall. This is *exactly* the point of the theology of the cross.

Therefore, Luther encouraged the study of Mary's teachings on this matter and encouraged the prince to be diligent in prayer in this manner: "Therefore, my Lord and Father, I ask that I be able to preside over these people to your honor and usefulness. Do not let me follow my own reason, but you be my reason."[22] Of course, this important teaching is for all people, not just rulers.

Mary concludes her teaching where her Magnificat began: with the Incarnation of the Son of God. When in Luke 1:54 Mary refers to God helping "his servant Israel," Luther wrote that the servant, whom the Incarnation of Christ benefits, refers to the people of Israel. In other words, Israel is God's "own beloved people for the sake of whom he became a human being, saves them from the power of the devil, sin, death, and hell and brings them to righteousness, eternal life, and salvation. That is the help of which Mary sings."[23] But "God has not helped Israel on the basis of merit, but on the basis of his promise. He made the promise out of pure grace, and he fulfilled it out of pure grace.... [Therefore,] the Mother of God praises and exalts this promise above everything else, attributing the Incarnation of God solely to the divine, gracious, undeserved promise God made to Abraham."[24]

This promise is not only for Israel. Luther ties Mary's reference to Abraham in Luke 1:55 to God's promise to Abraham in Genesis, when Luther commented on verse 55: "The promise of God to Abraham is recorded primarily in Genesis 12:3 and Genesis 22:18 and is referred to in many other places as well. It says: 'and in you all the families of the earth shall be blessed.'"[25] In this way, Luther understands the incorporation of Gentiles into the fulfillment of the promise made to Abraham. Therefore, in the Incarnation, God "raised up seed [i.e., the promised Messiah through whom all the families of the earth shall be blessed] from Abraham, the natural

21. See page 78.
22. See page 78.
23. See page 72.
24. See page 73.
25. See page 73.

son born to one of his daughters, a pure virgin, Mary, through the Holy Spirit, and without her lying with a man."[26] Luther wrote that in this seed of Abraham we have "the foundation of the Gospel." It is this foundation of which Mary sings—a foundation created by God's grace alone, and thus she sings: to God alone be the glory.

---

26. See page 74.

2

Introduction to Bach's *Magnificat*

THE MAGNIFICAT: BACH'S TWELVE MOVEMENTS IN LATIN AND TRANSLATED INTO ENGLISH

I. *Magnificat anima mea Dominum,*
My soul magnifies the Lord,

II. *Et exultavit spiritus meus in Deo salutari meo.*
And my spirit has rejoiced in God my Savior.

III. *Quia respexit humilitatem ancillae suae; ecce enim ex hoc . . . beatam me dicent.*
For he has regarded the lowliness of his handmaiden; for, behold, henceforth [all generations (See IV)] shall call me blessed.

IV. *Omnes generationes*
All generations

V. *Quia fecit mihi magna qui potens est, et sanctum nomen eius.*
For he that is mighty has done great things to me, and holy is his name.

VI. *Et misericordia eius a progenie in progenies timentibus eum.*
And his mercy is on them that fear him throughout all generations.

VII. *Fecit potentiam in brachio suo, dispersit superbos mente cordis sui.*
He has shown strength with his arm, and has scattered the proud in the imagination of their hearts.

VIII. *Deposuit potentes de sede, et exaltavit humiles.*
He has cast down the mighty from their seats, and exalted the lowly.

IX. *Esurientes implevit bonis, et divites dimisit inanes.*
He has filled the hungry with good things, and sent the rich away empty.

X. *Suscepit Israel puerum suum, recordatus misericordiae suae,*
He has helped his servant Israel, in remembrance of his mercy,

XI. *Sicut locutus est ad patres nostros, Abraham et semini eius in saecula.*
As he promised to our forefathers, to Abraham and his seed for ever.

XII. *Gloria patri, gloria Filio, gloria et Spiritui Sancto. Sicut erat in prinicipio, et nunc, et semper in saecula saeculorum. Amen*
Glory to the Father, glory to the Son, and glory to the Holy Spirit. As it was in the beginning, is now, and ever shall be, world without end. Amen.

THE MAGNIFICAT: CENTURIES OF INSPIRATION

The Magnificat ("My Soul Magnifies the Lord"), also known as the Song of Mary, the Canticle of Mary, and, in Byzantine Traditon, the Ode of the Theotokos,[1] is a canticle frequently sung liturgically in the Christian church. Its name comes from the first word—*magnificat*—of the Latin version of the canticle's text. From the Gospel of Luke (1:46–55), the text has been set to music almost more than any other text beside the Mass texts (liturgies of Holy Communion). Beginning with Gregorian chant, to the polyphonic settings of the Renaissance, to the concerted Magnificat settings with full orchestra, chorus, and soloists of the late Baroque/Classical era, to the present day, composers have been inspired and are still being inspired by this magnificent text.

As the Magnificat is part of the sung Vespers in Roman Catholic, Anglican, and Lutheran traditions, many composers have set the Magnificat for that purpose; for example, Claudio Monteverdi composed *Vespro della Beata Vergine* (Vespers for the Blessed Virgin) for soloists, choir, and orchestra in grand style for St. Mark's in Venice. Mozart included the Magnificat as the last movement of his *Solemn Vespers*. Together with the Nunc Dimittis (Song of Simeon, Luke 2:29–32), the Magnificat is a regular part of the Anglican Evensong.[2] The Magnificat and the Nunc Dimittis have been set to music by many famous English composers, such as Thomas Tallis and Ralph Vaughan Williams. It is so widely used that Charles Villiers Stanford wrote a set in every key and Herbert Howells composed twenty such settings in his career.

1. Greek for "bearer of God."
2. The name for Vespers in the Anglican tradition.

Introduction to Bach's *Magnificat*

The Magnificat text continues to inspire composers today. The late Romantic composer Anton Bruckner composed it for soloists, choir, orchestra, and organ. Into the twentieth and twenty-first centuries, Rachmaninoff and more recently John Rutter also made settings, inserting additions into the text. For example, Rutter inserted *Of a Rose, a Lovely Rose* and other texts in his composition. Contemporary Estonian composer Arvo Pärt set the text for an a cappella chorus. Even within the last decade or so, there are dozens of new settings of the Magnificat, including one with a tango touch by Argentinian composer Martin Palmeri, which includes the bandoneon, an accordion-like instrument especially used for tangos! Then, there is the *Magnificat* in E-flat by Johann Sebastian Bach, a work equal to the best of them.

BACH: LUTHER'S SPIRITUAL HEIR

The *Magnificat* in E-flat Major was composed in 1723, Bach's first year at his new position as cantor in Leipzig. Bach had never undertaken such a big project. Written for a large orchestra, five-part chorus, five soloists, and lasting half an hour, Bach's *Magnificat* is rich in interpreting the text through music. In order to understand Bach's musical language and the spirituality that accompanies it, it is important to explore his religious and spiritual background, particularly his familiarity with Martin Luther.

By all accounts, Bach was deeply religious. However, his professional responsibilities throughout his life included working for secular as well as religious authorities, and his surviving compositions reflect this career duality. The evidence reflected in his letters, in his professional trajectory, and in the very nature of his activities in liturgical composition and performance leave little reason to doubt his fundamental piety. There is little doubt, as well, that he was thoroughly Lutheran in his theology. If Bach might be thought of as a spiritual heir to Luther; some would even go further and stress an almost father-son relationship. As one author put it, "Luther clarified the faith and Bach set it to music."[3]

Even though they lived two centuries apart, the synergy between Bach and Luther can be seen in both geography and the coincidence of schooling.[4] Born in 1685 in Eisenach, Bach was immediately a participant in the life and theology of Luther. The baptismal font in the *Georgenkirche*

---

3. Tammen, "Why Did Bach, a Lutheran, Compose a Mass?"
4. Gardiner, *Music in a Castle of Heaven*, 25.

(Church of St. George), where Bach was baptized, is near the pulpit where Luther preached upon returning to Eisenach from Worms. Bach and Luther attended the same Latin school, where Bach studied Orthodox Lutheranism and Latin, among other subjects. As boys, both were choristers in the *Schulenchor*. While members of the choir, they even shared the extracurricular tradition of "busking for bread," choristers who went out singing in four-part harmony hoping for donations of some kind![5]

All this was reinforced by the important ways that Luther's hymns and theology were infused in Bach's schooling. For example, Bach's early cantatas illustrate Luther's late-medieval concept that life is a daily battle between God and Satan. In cantata #4, written for Easter in 1707, Bach uses Luther's hymn *Christ lag in Todesbanden* (Christ lay in death's bonds). In that chorale, and thus in the cantata, Bach portrays Luther's theological beliefs about Christ as both the conqueror of death and the sacrificial paschal lamb. One is to face death courageously. Bach scholars maintain that "his church music was grounded solely on Luther's teaching about the Word of God and of the essence of music."[6] Some scholars cite Luther's love of music and his assertion of its divine origin as the fundamental impulse behind Bach's work. Others say that the key to "opening the door on the whole world of Bach's innermost conceptions and ideas will be found in the writings of the reformer Martin Luther."[7] For Luther, next to the Word of God, only music deserves to be extolled as mistress and governess of human feelings. And, when music is sharpened and polished by art, then one begins to see with amazement the great and perfect wisdom of God in this wonderful work of harmony.[8] Thus music is there first and foremost to praise God. As Luther stated, quoting St. Augustine of Hippo,[9] "those who sing, pray twice."

Lutheranism thus involved a strong connection between Bible and hymn book and between pastor and cantor in the ecclesiastical culture of this era. A cantor such as Bach would have seen himself, and been seen as, a kind of musical pastor, with equal authority and responsibility. The

---

5. Luther admonished those who looked down on the *Currende* ("busking choristers"): "I, too was such a crumb collector . . . [we were singing and begging in four voices] from door to door, especially in my beloved city of Eisenach"(*LW* 46:250).

6. Lloyd, "Bach: Luther's Musical Prophet?," 5.

7. Leaver, "Bach and Luther," 9.

8. Bainton, *Here I Stand*, 352.

9. The name of a fifth-century bishop in North Africa.

Introduction to Bach's *Magnificat*

religious message and leadership were the same, the rhetoric of the preaching was the same, but the medium was music rather than speech.

When Bach was forty-eight years old, he acquired a copy of Luther's three-volume translation of the Bible. He pored over it as if it were a long-lost treasure. He underlined passages, corrected errors in the text and commentary, inserted missing words, and made notes in the margins.

Near 1 Chronicles 25, a listing of David's musicians, he wrote, "this chapter is the true foundation of all God-pleasing music." At 2 Chronicles 5:13, which speaks of temple musicians praising God, he wrote, "at a reverent performance of music, God is always at hand with his gracious pleasure." Bach was indeed a Christian who lived with the Bible. Moreover, he was a staunch Lutheran who was well versed in the doctrines of the Christian faith and owned eighty-three religious volumes, including Luther's greatest works.

In addition to being the greatest composer of the Baroque era, Bach is also considered today to be one of the musical geniuses in the history of Western music. In addition, he was a theologian who just happened to work with a keyboard. His musical genius, his devotion to Christ, and the effect of his music in worship led to his often being called the "fifth evangelist" (i.e., after Matthew, Mark, Luke, and John) because his cantatas during Sunday services were like a musical sermon.[10] At the end of his compositions, Bach wrote "SDG"—*Soli Deo gloria* (To God alone be the glory). Often at the beginning of his compositions, he would write "JJ," referring to *Jesu juban* (Help me, Jesus). Also, he offered many of his cantatas "I.N.J.," *In nomine Jesu* (In the name of Jesus).

On the subject of the Virgin Mary, Luther sees Mary as a lowly maid, a teacher, the Mother of God, and a demonstration of grace. For Luther, Mary is an example of how to live. His *Commentary*, written for a prince, is a warning that it is those who are lowly that God lifts up and those who are proud that God will scatter. The themes of exalting the humble, dashing those who are powerful and arrogant, magnifying God as the giver of great things, and filling the hungry with good things are themes that Bach echoes in his *Magnificat* with his own musical language. Albert Schweitzer wrote, "The structure of Bach's musical phrase does not merely fit more or less the structure of the poetic phrase, but is identical with it."[11] In essence, Bach takes a poem or text from Scripture and becomes one with it. His

---

10. Galli, "Fifth Evangelist."
11. Schweitzer, *J. S. Bach*, 1:25.

interpretation of the words is in his own musical language. In the *Magnificat* in E-flat, this amazing musical language comes to life in every single movement.

BACH'S MUSICAL LANGUAGE

In some ways, Bach's musical language was a product of his times. As an art form, Western music before Bach and Luther had been perceived as a mathematical discipline. The study of music was grounded in the *quadrivium*, a Latin word meaning "the four ways" or a "place where four roads meet." It consists of arithmetic, geometry, music, and astronomy. (Music in the *quadrivium* had more to do with harmonics, i.e., the mathematical proportion between musical intervals). The *quadrivium* along with the *trivium*, which consists of the "thinking skills" of grammar, logic, and rhetoric, make up the seven liberal arts, derived from Plato's educational curriculum outlined in his *Republic*. During the Renaissance, the study of music began to shift away from the mathematical intervals and towards the linguistic and humanistic disciplines of the *trivium*, particularly rhetoric. Luther's posting of the 95 Theses, the beginning of the Reformation, corresponds to this rise of using rhetoric as a basis for music composition. Luther's view of music was that it was not merely a beautiful art form, but rather ranked "next to theology." Dating back as far as 1537, there is evidence of Lutheranism's musical connections to rhetoric. In that year Nicolaus Listenius, a Wittenberg schoolmaster and Lutheran musician and theologian, wrote the textbook *Musica*. Primarily a primer for music composition, it became widely used in German and Austrian classrooms. *Musica theoretica* and *musica practica* (the theory and practice of music) were common phrases in the study of music. Alongside these two, Listenius coined the phrase *musica poetica*,[12] by which he meant the study of composition in relation to sound, structure, and the meaning of a text. Bach's early education probably included the textbook *Musica*. His link to the rhetorical practice and application in music may also have been influenced by his friendship with Abraham Birnbaum, professor of rhetoric at the University of Leipzig. Thus, Bach's compositional style had a firm foundation in rhetoric. In his religious music particularly, Bach was not only composing music but also teaching and preaching the Word of God, operating as a kind of musical pastor.

12. Listenius, *Rudimenta musica*.

Introduction to Bach's *Magnificat*

In addition to the use of rhetoric, the musical culture of Bach and his contemporaries also included numerology, musical puzzles, and symbolism. Books and music published throughout the Baroque era showed the use of symbolism and numerology, mostly for "fun," but also for the purpose of demonstrating a composer's compositional prowess. One example is Bach's organ work, *Dies sind die Heil'gen Zehn Gebot* (These are the holy Ten Commandments). When the main theme occurs, a single note is repeated ten times, connecting it to the title. Also, the use of musical cryptography in the time of Bach meant encoding references in a composition to something like a composer's name. One of Bach's well-known fugues, *Mass in B minor*, is based on the notes B-flat, A, C, and B natural. In the German tradition, B stands for the note B-flat, whereas B natural is written as H. The German title of this work is *Messe in h-moll*. Therefore, encrypted in the fugue's subject are the letters B-A-C-H. Another example is Johann Jacob Froberger's keyboard composition written for Emperor Frederick III's supposed ascension to heaven. It is based on an F major scale (F as in Frederick). In it the ascending melodic line peaks on an F repeated three times—as if Frederick III is floating in the clouds with the Trinity!

Likewise, Bach's choice of the key of E-flat major for his *Magnificat* was probably not an accident. In the seventeenth and eighteenth centuries, *Affektenlehre*, the rhetorical "doctrine of affections" or the "doctrine of passions,"[13] was widely used in the aesthetics of music, art, and theater. The doctrine arose from ancient theories of rhetoric and oratory and was used as a pattern for music composition. It was an elaborate theory based on the idea that passions could be represented by their outward or visible signs. In a 1694 treatise, René Descartes held that there were six basic affects or passions: *admiration* (admiration), *amour* (love), *haine* (hatred), *désir* (desire), *joie* (joy), and *tristesse* (sorrow).[14] Other lists in writings of the time included many more than just these six, but these "affections" were not a display of emotions. Rather, the affect referred to the "spiritual movement of the mind." Each musical key related to an affect. For example, the key of C major is "completely pure," with a character of innocence and simplicity. The character of the key of E minor is both a declaration of love as well as a lament "without grumbling"—sighs with a few tears. Written in the key of E minor, *Jesu meine Freude*, one of Bach's first Leipzig compositions, was a

---

13. Mattheson, *Das neu-eröffnete orchestre*.
14. Descartes, *Les passions de l'ame*.

funeral motet. E minor also speaks of the imminent hope of resolving into pure happiness in the key of C major.[15]

The *Magnificat*'s key of E-flat major included various affects. First, the key is of love, devotion, and intimate conversation with God. Mary's humility towards God in her own words demonstrates love and devotion. The other aspect of E-flat major is that it is a heroic key, full of majestic seriousness and gravity.[16] (Later, as the use of *Affektenlehre* was dwindling in the Classical era, Beethoven nevertheless chose the key of E-flat major for one of his most majestic compositions, his third symphony, the *Eroica*, written in honor of Napoleon Bonaparte.) Bach's *Magnificat* in E-flat Major has aspects of both affections. Mary's words of humility and reverence are an intimate conversation with God. At the same time, the opening and closing of his *Magnificat* exude nothing but joy and majesty!

With the introductions to Luther's commentary and Bach's *Magnificat* presented in chapters 1 and 2, respectively, we are prepared to turn to the new translation of Luther's commentary in its entirety.

---

15. Schubart, *Ideen zu einter Aesthetik der Tonkunst.*
16. Mattheson, *Der Vollkommene Capellmeister.*

3

Luther's *Commentary on the Magnificat*

THE MAGNIFICAT

Translated into German and interpreted by

DR. MARTIN LUTHER
1521

A new translation into English by

DR. RANDI H. LUNDELL
2014

Luther's *Commentary on the Magnificat*

LETTER OF DEDICATION TO PRINCE JOHN FREDERICK

To His Serene Highness, Prince John Frederick, Duke of Saxony, Landgrave of Thuringia, Margrave of Meissen, My Gracious Lord and Patron. Serene and High-Born Prince, gracious lord! Please accept my humble prayer and service as always.

Your Grace, I recently received your letter and its cheerful contents made me very glad. A long time ago I promised you a work on the Magnificat, but am guilty of allowing myself to be interrupted by the troublesome quarrels of many adversaries. So I have decided to respond with this small book, since if I put it off any longer I will turn red with embarrassment. And it is not acceptable for me to make any more excuses which might dampen your youthful spirit, which is inclined to love the Holy Scriptures and which by further study of them might be all the more engaged and strengthened. To this end I wish God's grace and help on your behalf.

And the need is very great, for the welfare of many lies with the power of such a mighty prince, if he goes beyond himself to be graciously ruled by God, just as, on the other hand, the ruin of many lies in his power, if he relies on himself and is ruled by God's disfavor. For while the hearts of all people are in God's almighty hand, it is for good reason that it is said primarily of kings and princes, "The king's heart is a stream of water in the hand of the Lord; he turns it wherever he will" (Proverbs 21:1). In other words, God wants to instill his fear in the mighty lords and teach them that all their thoughts and intentions amount to nothing without his unique inspiration. Other people's actions bring gain or loss only upon themselves or maybe on a few others, but rulers are appointed for the particular purpose of being able to either harm or help others—and the larger the population, the more extensive their domain. Thus the Scriptures also call pious and God-fearing princes angels of God and even gods; but it calls harmful princes lions, dragons, and wild beasts, which God includes among his four plagues—pestilence, famine, war, and enraged beasts (Revelation 6:1–8). Accordingly, the heart, being by nature but flesh and blood, is prone to arrogance. When, in addition, a prince achieves power, riches, and honor, these things form such a strong incentive to presumption and overconfidence as to cause him to forget God and not care about his subjects. And because he is also able to do wrong with impunity, he lets himself go and becomes a beast, does whatever he pleases, and is a ruler in name, but a monster in deed. As the sage Bias[1] said, *Magistratus virum ostendit*: the office of ruler reveals what manner of man the ruler is and his subjects dare not let themselves go for fear of the authorities. Therefore since all rulers do not need to fear people, they should fear God more than other people do and should learn to know him and his works, and to walk with care, as St. Paul says in Romans 12:8: "He that rules, let him do it with diligence."

Now I do not know of anything else in the Scriptures that serves such a purpose as well as does this sacred hymn of the most blessed Mother of God, which should be learned and reflected on by all who want to rule well and desire to be helpful lords. Truly, she sings most sweetly of the fear of God, what kind of Lord he is, and especially of how he deals with those of high and of low status. Let another listen to a worldly love song; this pure Virgin deserves to be heard by a prince and lord as she sings her sacred, chaste, and holy song. It is also a good custom that this canticle is sung daily in all the churches at vespers, and in a particular and appropriate setting that distinguishes it from the other canticles. May the tender Mother of God herself give me the spirit of wisdom to ably and thoroughly expound on this song of hers so that you, as well as the rest of us, may all gain by it saving knowledge and a praiseworthy life, and praise and sing this Magnificat through all eternity. So help us God. Amen.

I now commend myself to your Grace, humbly praying that your Grace will receive my feeble attempt in all kindness.

Your Grace's obedient chaplain,
Dr. Martin Luther
Wittenberg, March 10, 1521

---

1. Bias of Priene was one of the "Seven Sages" of Greece. He lived during the sixth century BC.

Luther's *Commentary on the Magnificat*

COMMENTARY ON THE MAGNIFICAT

In order to fully understand this sacred song of praise, we must realize that the Virgin Mary is speaking about her own very personal experience, one that was inspired and informed by the Holy Spirit, since no one can correctly understand God or his Word unless they are led by the Holy Spirit. By the same token, no one can receive God's Word through the Holy Spirit unless they experience it, test it, and feel it. When we experience it, the Holy Spirit instructs us as if we were attending his own school, outside of which everything else is mere chatter and nonsense. When the Virgin Mary experienced for herself that God had plans to do great things through her, despite the fact that she was of humble origin, plain, poor, and lowly, the Holy Spirit revealed to her his rich insight and wisdom that God is a God who sees fit to elevate the lowly and to bring down the mighty and powerful; in short, he is a God who breaks apart what is whole and makes whole what is broken.

Just as in the beginning of the world God created all creatures of the world from nothing because he is "creator" and "almighty," he is always constant in how he does things. All of his works, to the very end of the world, are created in such a way that he makes something valuable, honorable, holy, and alive from something that was nothing, lowly, despised, paltry, and dead. By the same token, he makes everything that was valuable, honorable, holy, and alive into nothing, into something small, despised, paltry, and dead. No creature is able to make something out of nothing like God can. Thus, God's eyes look only into the depths and not toward the heights, as Daniel says in the story of the three men in the oven in Daniel 3:55 (Vulgate[2]): "You sit upon the cherubim and behold the depths," and in Psalm 138, verse 6: "Though the Lord is on high, he looks upon the lowly; but the proud he knows from afar." And in Psalm 113, verse 5: "Who is like the Lord our God, who is seated on high, who looks far down on the heavens and the earth?" For since he is the Almighty and nothing is above him, he therefore cannot look above himself; he also cannot look to either side, for there is nothing like him. Since nothing is like him, he must necessarily look within and beneath himself, so that the lower one is, the better God is able to see him.

But the world and the eyes of people do the opposite; they look upward and want to elevate themselves, as it says in Proverbs 30:13: "Those

---

2. The Vulgate is a Latin translation of the Bible.

whose eyes are ever so haughty, whose glances are so disdainful." We see this on a daily basis, how people strive for honor, power, riches, knowledge, a life of comfort, and whatever is considered the best and greatest. And wherever these kinds of people are, there are hangers-on who fawn over them and who willingly serve them; who want to be like them and share in their glory. It is therefore no wonder that the Bible describes very few kings and nobles as godly men. By contrast, nobody likes to look into the depths where there are poverty, disgrace, squalor, anguish, and fear; people turn their eyes away from such things. And wherever they come upon such people, they run the other way and avoid them; they leave them be and no one thinks to help them, to live among them, or to help them better themselves. So they stay in the depths of despair, in their lowly and despised condition. There is no creator among people who can make something from nothing, as Paul teaches in Romans 12:16, where he says: "Do not be proud, but be willing to associate with people of low position. Do not be conceited."

God is the only one who has the kind of sight that looks into the depths of misery and anguish, and is near to everyone who is in the depths of despair, as 1 Peter 5:5 says: "'God opposes the proud, but gives grace to the humble.'" This then is the source of humankind's ability to love and praise God, for no one can praise God who has not first loved him. Furthermore, no one can love God unless God reveals himself as loving and caring, and he cannot be revealed to us except through his works which he shows forth through us, and which we feel and experience. Wherever it is experienced that he is the kind of God who looks down into the depths and helps only the poor, dejected, suffering, miserable, and abandoned, and those who are nothing, there he has the love of people whose hearts overflow with joy, leaping and dancing with gladness that they have found God. Such is the work of the Holy Spirit who, in the blink of an eye, gives us such amazing knowledge and joy through this experience.

Therefore, God has condemned us all to death and laid the cross of Christ, along with immeasurable suffering and anguish, on his dear children and Christians. He even allows us at times to fall into sin so that he can look into the depths and help many people, perform many works, and show himself as a true Creator, making himself known as loving and worthy of praise. Unfortunately, without fail the world resists him in this in its short-sightedness and prevents his seeing, working, and helping, robbing him of his honor, as well as his pleasure, joy, and salvation. So he sent his only beloved son Jesus Christ into the depths of all misery and through him

Luther's *Commentary on the Magnificat*

exemplified the goal to which his seeing, works, help, methods, counsel, and will are directed. Thus, having most fully experienced these attributes of God, Christ remains for all eternity in the knowledge, love, and praise of God. As it says in Psalm 21:6: "You make him glad with the joy of your presence," namely, in that God sees you and knows you. And in Psalm 44:7 and 8, it says the saints do nothing else in heaven but praise God's name all day long because he saw them in the depths and revealed himself to them, eliciting their love and praise.

The tender Mother of Christ does the same thing here (in this song of praise). She teaches us, using words and the example of her experience, how one can know, love, and praise God. Because she praises God here with a happy and joyous spirit and declares that he has seen her, despite the fact that she is poor and from nothing, one must conclude that her parents were poor, despised, and lowly. In order to make it as simple as possible, there were undoubtedly daughters of priests and lawyers in Jerusalem as well as in many other cities who were rich, good looking, young, well-educated, and held in high esteem across the land (as are today the daughters of kings, princes, and wealthy people). Even in her home town of Nazareth she was not the daughter of a chief ruler, but a simple poor man's daughter, whom no one regarded very highly or paid any attention to. To her neighbors and their daughters she was a simple girl who tended the cattle and did chores around the house; no doubt she would be regarded in today's world as a domestic servant who does what she is told.

Isaiah 11:1 and 2 says: "A shoot will come up from the stump of Jesse; from his roots a Branch will bear fruit." The shoot and the root is the generation of Jesse, or David, specifically the Virgin Mary; the rod and the flower is Christ. Just as it was impossible to foresee and to believe that from such a scrawny, withered stem and root such a fair twig and branch would spring, so it was also just as impossible to foresee that Mary, the virgin, would be the mother of such a child. For I believe that she is not only called a shoot and a root because she became a mother in a miraculous way without losing her virginity (just as it is miraculous that a shoot should grow from a dead tree stump), but also because she is of the royal stem and line of David, which, during the time of David and Solomon, had flourished in terms of honor, power, riches, and fortune in the eyes of the world. But toward the end, when Christ was about to come, the priests had taken over this honor and ruled everything, and the line of David was impoverished and dejected like a dead tree stump so that there was no hope or indication that a king who descended from it would ever achieve greatness. And when things seemed to be at their worst, along comes Christ, born of the despised stump—of a poor, lowly maiden! The branch and the flower grow from a person whom the daughter of Annas or Caiaphas would never have considered good enough to hire as a lowly lady's maid. Thus, God looks into the depths and does his work there, while the eyes of people and their ambitions only look up. This is the context for Mary's canticle, which we will now interpret line by line.

I. My soul glorifies the Lord (v. 46).

These words express the complete joy and exuberance of a mind and an internal life buoyed up by the spirit. That is why she does not say, "I praise the Lord," but rather "my soul" praises him, as if to say, "my entire life and all of my senses hover in the love, praise, and lofty bliss of God so that I am no longer in charge of myself and am raised to a state of praising God quite apart from my own volition." This happens to everyone who is filled with the divine sweetness of the Spirit; they feel much more than they are able to express. People are not capable of praising God with gladness by themselves, but it is more like a joyful burden laid on them only by God that cannot be expressed in words, but is learned through individual experience. As David says in Psalm 34:8: "Taste and see that the Lord is good; blessed is the one who takes refuge in him." He first has us taste and then see because we cannot fathom it unless we have experienced it and felt it for ourselves, and we do not reach that point unless we trust God with our whole heart when we are in the depths of need and despair. That is why David adds: "Blessed is the one who trusts in the Lord," for this person will experience God at work in his life and will sense his sweetness and thus be granted knowledge and understanding. Let us now look at the text in detail.

The first words are "my soul." Scripture divides a person into three parts, as Paul says in 1 Thessalonians 5:23: "May the God of peace himself sanctify you entirely; and may your spirit, soul, and body be kept sound and blameless at the coming of our Lord Jesus Christ." And each part, together with the whole person, is further divided into two parts: spirit and flesh. This is not a division of the nature of the person, but of the person's characteristics. This means that human nature is divided into three parts: spirit, soul, and body, each of which can be either good or bad, namely, spirit or flesh, but that is not the topic of discussion here.

Luther's *Commentary on the Magnificat*

The first part, the spirit, is the highest, deepest, and most noble part of the person by which this person is able to grasp things that are incomprehensible, invisible, and eternal. It is, in short, the place where faith and God's Word reside. As David says in Psalm 51:10: "Create in me a clean heart, O God, and put a new and right spirit within me," namely, a true and strong faith. On the other hand, he says in Psalm 78:37: "Their heart was not steadfast toward him; they were not true to his covenant."

The second part, the soul, is similar in nature to spirit, but in a different way, namely, it gives life to the body and works through the body and is often referred to in the Scriptures as "life." For the soul can exist without the body, but the body cannot exist without the soul. We see how this part is unceasingly at work, even when we sleep. Its job is not to comprehend the incomprehensible, but to know and assess using reason. Reason is the light in the house, and unless the spirit, which is able to enlighten with the brighter light of faith, rules reason, it will always be wrong because it is too weak to deal with divine things. The Scriptures attribute many things to these two parts of people, such as wisdom and knowledge, the wisdom of the spirit, the knowledge of the soul; but it also attributes hate, love, passion, horror, and the like.

The third part is the body with its members; its activity is to carry out and use what the soul knows and the spirit believes. To make a comparison using Scripture, we read that Moses built the tabernacle in three separate parts. The first part was called the "holy of holies," the dwelling place of God where there was no light. The second part was called the "holy place," which contained a candlestick with seven arms and seven lamps. The third place was called the "courtyard," which lay under the open sky and in the sunlight. People are fashioned in the same way: one's spirit is the holy of holies, where God dwells in faith's darkness where there is no light because one can only believe what one does not see, feel, or grasp. One's soul is the holy place with its seven lamps, representing all forms of reason, discernment, knowledge, and understanding of physical, visible things. One's body is the courtyard, obvious to all, so that one can see the person's deeds and how the person lives.

In 1 Thessalonians 5:23, Paul asks God, who is a God of peace, to make not just one part of us holy, but the whole person, through and through, so that spirit, soul, body, and everything are holy. Much could be said about the reason for such a prayer, but, in short, if the spirit is not holy then nothing else is holy. The holiness of the spirit is the source of the greatest conflict and danger because it consists of sheer, pure faith, since the spirit does not deal with comprehensible things, as we have said. Therefore false teachers come along and set up decoys for the spirit: this one with works, the other with the way to attain holiness. But if the spirit is not protected and prudent, it will stray and follow these false teachers and rely on external works and ways, thinking that it can attain holiness through them, and soon all faith will be lost and the spirit will be dead in the sight of God.

Next, there are the various sects and orders. One man becomes a Carthusian,[3] and another a Franciscan,[4] thinking that with fasting and prayer, or by other works, they will be saved. These orders and works were never commanded by God, but were invented by people so that they will not have need of faith. Meanwhile, they teach people to rely on works so that finally, mired deep in works, they begin to disagree among themselves, claiming that they are the greatest and having contempt for others, like the Caramelites[5] do today with their bragging and boasting. Paul admonishes against such saints of works-righteousness and supposedly pious teachers, saying that God is a God of peace and unity who will not have or hold such divided and contentious saints. They must give up their ways and come together in the spirit and in faith and realize that works only create divisions and make for sin and discord, while only faith makes people pious, united, and peaceable. As it says in Psalm 133:1: "How good and pleasant it is when brothers dwell in unity!"

Peace comes in another way where one teaches that no work, no external method, but only faith makes one pious, righteous, and holy, giving us confidence in the promised, invisible grace of God, about which I have spoken at length in my *Treatise on Good Works*. Where there is no faith, there must be many works, which are followed by discord and divisions, chasing God away. Thus, Paul does not say in 1 Thessalonians 5:23 only "your spirit and soul," but rather "your whole spirit." It all depends on the spirit. It is as if to say: "Do not let works lead you astray; a believing spirit is all you need." Everything rests on a believing spirit, and I pray that God preserves in you "a spirit that possesses the entire inheritance" to protect you from false doctrines that teach our trust in God is based on works. But these

---

3. The Carthusian monastic order was founded by Bruno of Cologne in 1084.

4. The Franciscan monastic order was founded on the spiritual disciplines of St. Francis of Assisi (1182–1226).

5. The Carmelite monastic order was founded around 1200 on Mount Carmel in Israel.

are false teachings because their trust is not built on God's grace alone. However, when the spirit "that is your entire inheritance" is preserved, then both body and soul can remain without error and evil works. Otherwise, it is very possible that where the spirit is without faith, the soul and the entire life goes astray and errs, even though it may have good intentions and say kind things, but as a result is completely satisfied with itself. With such errors and false "good intentions," the soul and all works of the body are evil and condemned, even if a person fasts himself to death and does works equal to those of the saints. That is why it is necessary for God to preserve first our spirit and then our soul and body, so that we do not strive or live in vain, but become truly holy and free not only from outward sin, but even more from false and seemingly good works.

Let this then conclude the clarification of "soul" and "spirit" because they appear frequently elsewhere in Scripture. Next comes the word "magnify," which means to "make great," to "lift up," to "highly esteem"; to regard as one who is capable of many great things, knowledge, and power, like those mentioned in this song. In the same way that the title of a book indicates what the contents are, the word "magnify" is used by Mary to indicate what her hymn of praise will be about: the great and mighty works of God, in order to strengthen our faith, to comfort those in need, and to terrify all the powerful people on earth. We should therefore understand this hymn from these three vantage points or purposes because Mary did not sing it just for her own benefit, but for ours as well, so that we could sing it after her. A person will not fear or be comforted by these great works of God unless one first believes that God has the power and knowledge to do such great things. However, one must also believe that God wants to do them and does them out of love. And it is also not sufficient that you believe that he does great works only for others and not for you, making you an exception from his divine works, as do those who do not fear God because they are powerful or as those who lose heart because of their problems.

Such faith is nothing and dead, like something in a fairy tale, but you must constantly keep his will for you in view and believe, beyond any doubt or wavering, that he will and can do great things in you. Such faith lives and moves; it penetrates and changes the entire person. It compels fear in the mighty and comforts the lowly. The higher and mightier you are, the more you must fear; and the lowlier you are, the more you must be comforted by this faith that is unlike any other. How will you behave in the hour of death? You must not only believe that God has the power and knowledge to help you, but also that he wants to, for it is an unspeakably great work to save you from eternal death and make you eternally blessed and God's heir. For this kind of faith, all things are possible, as Christ says (Mark 9:23), and it alone abides. This kind of faith also experiences God's works and through them the love of God, singing praises to God, thus glorifying and magnifying him.

We cannot make God great, for his nature is unchangeable, but rather through our understanding and experience we are led to regard him highly and esteem him because of his goodness and mercy. Therefore the Holy Mother does not say "my voice," or "my mouth," and also not "my hand," or "my thoughts," or "my reason," or "my will" magnifies the Lord. For there are many who praise God with a loud voice, preach about him eloquently, read a lot about him, discuss and write about him, and try to paint a picture of him. There are many who reflect upon him and who by means of their reason aspire to speculate about him, as well as those who elevate him with a false devotion and intent. But Mary says: "My soul magnifies the Lord," meaning that her entire life and being, mind, and strength regard him highly, so that she feels transported and elevated by his gracious goodness, as the next verse shows. Here it is like when someone does something particularly nice for us, causing our whole being to be inclined toward him and we respond by saying: "I highly regard him," which really means, my soul magnifies him. How much more will such a feeling reign in us when we experience God's goodness, which is exceedingly great in all of its aspects, so that all our words and thoughts are too insufficient and our entire life and soul are compelled to express themselves, as though everything in us wanted to break out in praise and song?

There are two kinds of false spirits that cannot sing the Magnificat appropriately: the first is those who will not praise him unless he gives them only good things, like David says in Psalm 49:18: "People praise you when they prosper." These people seem to praise God, but because they are not willing to suffer oppression or be in the depths, they cannot experience the works of God and therefore are not able to truly love or praise God. Thus the world is full of worship services and praise with singing, preaching, organ playing, and trumpets, as well as wonderful performances of the Magnificat. It is a pity that such a wonderful canticle should be sung without any salt or savor and that we only recite it when things are going well, but when things are not going well the singing stops and we no longer think highly of God but think that he can or will do nothing for us. When that happens, the Magnificat is left out.

The other kind of false spirit is even more dangerous because it errs on the other side, elevating itself by means of God's works and not ascribing them solely to his goodness alone. It wants to take credit for them and be set above others because of them. It looks at the gifts that God has given, clutching at them as if it had earned them all on its own and feeling special in comparison to its needier neighbors. This is a slippery slope indeed. God's good gifts will quite naturally produce proud and conceited hearts, which is why it is important to note here that the last word is "God." Mary does not say: "My soul magnifies itself," or "regards itself highly." She does not point to herself here, but rather the glory all goes to God, who alone deserves it. She removes herself from view and draws all of the attention toward God, from whom she has received everything. For after experiencing such a momentous visit from God, she was in no frame of mind to try to elevate herself above the lowliest person on earth, since if she had done so she would have fallen, like Lucifer, into the darkest abyss of hell (Isaiah 14:12).

She thought only this: If any other girl had received such goodness from God, she would be just as happy as I am and would not begrudge me this joy. Indeed, Mary felt that she was uniquely unworthy and that all others were more worthy. Furthermore, she would have been very content if God had taken back his blessing and given it to another girl before her very eyes, so completely did she give up her claim to anything, leaving all good gifts freely, simply, and appropriately in God's hands, considering herself nothing more than a happy hostel and willing waitress for such a guest. Therefore she kept this in mind forever, namely, to give God alone the glory, to magnify only him, and to give ourselves credit for nothing. At this point, it is not hard to see how easy it would be for her to fall into sin, so that it is no less a miracle that she kept her pride and arrogance at bay when she received these gifts. Can you imagine what a wonderful heart that is? She finds herself elevated above all other people as the Mother of God and yet remains so simple and serene that she does not think of herself above the very lowliest of serving girls. Oh, we are such poor mortals that when we receive some degree of wealth, power, or honor, if perhaps we are even just a bit nicer looking than others, we cannot help but compare ourselves to others less fortunate and there is no end to our self-aggrandizement. What will we do then when we receive greater, higher gifts?

As a result, God lets us stay poor and unlucky because we cannot help but taint his wonderful gifts and cannot (when we acknowledge them) think of ourselves thus as before (when we did not have them), but our mood rises and falls when the gifts come and go. Mary's heart, on the other hand, remains firm and steady the whole time, allows God to work according to his will, and takes her only comfort, joy, and trust in God. This is how we should be too, if we want to sing the Magnificat in the right spirit.

II. And my spirit rejoices in God, my Savior (v. 47).

We have already talked about what the spirit is; through faith it helps us comprehend the incomprehensible. Therefore Mary calls God her "Savior" or "Salvation," although she could not see him or feel him, nevertheless, she firmly trusts him with all confidence that he is her Savior and Salvation. This faith she received by means of the work that God had done in her. Indeed, in correct order she calls God "Lord" before calling him "Savior," and calls him "Savior" before listing all of his works. Accordingly, she teaches us to love and praise God for himself alone and not merely seek what we want from him. The person who loves and praises God appropriately is the person who praises him solely because he is good and sees nothing more than his pure goodness, and only on that account is joyful and glad. That is the lofty, pure, and tender way to love and to praise God exemplified in the Virgin Mary's lofty and tender spirit.

However, there are the foul and perverted lovers who are nothing more than self-seeking, who look to God out of self-interest and do not praise and love his pure goodness, but only think of themselves and how good God has been to them and of how much they can demonstrate his goodness to them and what he has done for them. They esteem him highly, are happy, and sing about and praise him as long as this feeling lasts. But when God hides himself and retracts the luster of his goodness, leaving them bereft and miserable, then their love and praise dry up and they are not able to either love or praise the pure, imperceptible, hidden goodness of God. Thus, they prove that their spirit did not rejoice in God their Savior. They did not love and praise his pure goodness, but were more interested in salvation than in their Savior, more in the gift than the Giver, and more interested in creaturely things than in their Creator. They cannot remain constant in need and desperation, in both wealth and poverty, as Paul says in Philippians 4:12: "I have learned the secret of being content in any and every situation, whether well fed or hungry, whether living in plenty or in want."

Psalm 49:18 reads: "People praise you when you prosper," as if to say: "They congratulate themselves, and not you, when they receive good and pleasant things." They never quit, as Christ says in John 6:26 to those who seek him: "I tell you the truth, you are looking for me, not because you saw miraculous signs but because you ate the loaves and had your fill." Such defiled, false spirits sully all of God's gifts and prevent him from giving them good things, especially working in them the gift of salvation.

A story best illustrates this. Long ago a pious woman had a vision of three virgins sitting near an altar. During Mass a good-looking young boy ran from the altar and approached the first virgin in a friendly way, caressed her, and smiled lovingly at her. He then approached the second virgin and was not as friendly to her, nor did he caress her, but he did raise her veil and gave her a smile. He was not at all friendly to the third virgin. He struck her in the face, tussled with her, shoved her in the most unpleasant way, then ran quickly back to the altar and disappeared. The vision was interpreted for the woman as follows: The first virgin stands for the defiled, self-seeking spirits who want God to give them good things and to do their bidding more than they want to do his will. They do not want to suffer any misfortune, but constantly want their desires and need for comfort met by God and are not satisfied with his goodness alone. The second virgin represents the spirits who have begun to serve God and lack some things, but are not entirely bereft and still seek their own comfort and self-interest. God must now and then give them a loving look and allow them to sense his goodness, so that they thereby can learn to love and praise his pure goodness. The third virgin, the poor Cinderella, has nothing but misery and hardship, seeks nothing for herself, but is content to know that God is good, even if she never experiences it, something that seems impossible. In both instances she remains the same; she loves and praises God for his goodness both when she senses it and when she does not. She does not cling to his blessings when she has them, nor does she fall away when blessings are absent from her life. She is the true bride of Christ who says: "I do not seek what you have, but I seek you. I do not love you any more when things are going well or any less when they are not going well." Such spirits fulfill what is written in Isaiah 30:21: "And when you turn to the right or when you turn to the left, your ears shall hear a word behind you, saying:

'This is the way; walk in it,'" which means you should appropriately love and praise God with constancy and not seek your own self-interest or needs.

David was such a spirit. When he was cast out of Jerusalem by his son Absalom and found himself in danger of being forever exiled and never again being king or having God's favor, he said (2 Samuel 15:25–26): "If I find favor in the eyes of the Lord, he will bring me back and let me see it both it [the ark of God] and the place where it stays. But if he says, 'I take no pleasure in you,' here I am, let him do to me what seems good to him." Oh, what a pure spirit it is that does not stop praising, loving, and following God's goodness even in times of distress! Mary the Mother of God is also such a spirit who, though in the midst of such exceedingly great gifts, does not cling to them or seek her own interests, but maintains a pure spirit in her love and praise of the pure goodness of God, ready and willing even to accept God's withdrawal of his goodness from her, leaving her a poor, naked, wretched spirit.

Now, it is much more dangerous to try to temper oneself when one is rich and has great power and status than when one is poor, full of shame, and weak, since wealth, power, and status provide a powerful incentive and opportunity for doing evil. Therefore it is even more amazing to consider Mary's wonderful, pure spirit here where she receives such an overwhelming honor and does not allow herself to be tempted by it, but acts as if she does not even notice. She remains constant and set on the straight path. She clings only to divine goodness, which she can neither see nor touch, ignores the gifts that she can perceive, taking no delight in them, and does not seek her own interests, so that she is able to sing with a true voice: "My spirit rejoices in God, my Savior." Hers is truly a spirit that springs and leaps from faith, not because of God's perceptible gifts to her, but on account of God himself whom she does not perceive, and she is happy because of her salvation, which she only knows through faith. Such are the truly lowly, destitute, hungry, and God-fearing spirits, whom we shall discuss next.

From this we can know and judge how full the world is of false preachers and saints who preach about good works to all of the pitiable. Although there are some who preach correctly about how to do good works (as described above), the majority preach human doctrines and works that they have devised and erected. Unfortunately, even the best of them are still quite far from the "straight and narrow" road, so that they lead people astray, teaching them to do good works and lead a good life not for the sake of God's pure goodness, but for their own benefit. For they would abandon God's goodness without expressing any love or praise if there were no heaven or hell and if God's good gifts did not hold any advantage for them. These people are mere egomaniacs and hirelings; they are slaves, not sons; aliens, not heirs. They see themselves as idols whom God should love and praise, and want him to do for them what they should do for him. They have no spirit and God is not their Savior, but their things are their savior, by means of which God must serve them like a servant. These are the children of Israel, who were not satisfied with bread from heaven in the wilderness, but wanted meat, onions, and garlic, too (Numbers 11:4–35).

Unfortunately, the whole world, all of the monasteries, and all of the churches are filled with these types of people who go around with their false, perverted, and unsound spirit, urging and pushing others to be like them. And they esteem their good works so highly that they think they deserve heaven because of them. However, above all, the pure goodness of God should be preached and known, and we should know that God saves us out of his pure goodness, without receiving credit for good works. Therefore we, in turn, should look for deeds without any agenda of reward or benefit to ourselves and do them because of the pure goodness of God, desiring nothing more than his good will and giving no thought to reward, since the reward will come on its own without our having to seek it. For though it is possible that the reward will not follow when we act in a pure, right spirit without seeking any benefit or reward, God will not tolerate a self-seeking, impure spirit, and such a person will never receive a reward. A son as heir serves his father willingly without payment and for the sake of the father, and in the case where a child serves the father only for the sake of an inheritance, that child is utterly despicable and deserves to be disinherited.

III. For he has been mindful of the humble state of his servant. From now on all generations will call me blessed (v. 48).

Many people have translated the word *humilitas* as "humility," as if the Virgin Mary were promoting her own humility and boasting of it. As a result, many prelates have called themselves "*Humiliati*," which is very far from the truth, since no one can boast of any good thing in the sight of God without sin and perdition. In his sight one should not boast of anything else but his pure goodness and mercy, which he shows to us unworthy people, so that nothing of ours, but only God's love and praise, is in us and preserves us, as Solomon teaches in Proverbs 25:6–7: "Do not exalt yourself in the king's presence and do not claim a place among the great; it is better for him to say to you, 'Come up here,' than for him to humiliate you in the presence of a noble." How can we attribute such arrogance and pride to this pure, upright virgin that we would have her boast to God of her own humility, the highest of all the virtues? No one boasts of their own humility unless they are extremely arrogant. God alone knows humility, judges it, and reveals it, so that the person who is truly humble is least aware of it.

In scriptural usage, "to humble" means to "bring down" and "humiliate," so that Christians in many places in Scripture are referred to as *pauperes, afflicti, humiliati*, or "poor," "afflicted," "despised" people, as in Psalm 116:10: "'I am greatly afflicted.'" "Humility," therefore, is nothing other than a despised, scorned, lowly creature or position, such as the poor, sick, hungry, thirsty, the prisoners, the suffering and dying, like Job in his sufferings, David in his expulsion from the kingdom, and Christ, as well as all Christians, in their times of distress. Those are the depths of which were spoken above, into which only God's eyes look, while people look to the heights, that is, to what is deemed valuable, glistens, and is magnificent. Therefore in the Scriptures (Zechariah 12:4), Jerusalem is called a city upon which God's eyes are directed, meaning that Christianity is in the depths and despised by the world while God keeps her in his sights and his eyes are always fixed upon her, as it says in Psalm 32:8: "I will counsel you with my eye upon you."

Paul also says in 1 Corinthians 1:27–28: "But God chose what is foolish in the world to shame the wise; God chose is weak in the world to shame the strong; God chose what is low and despised in the world, things that are not, to reduce to nothing the things that are." And so he makes the wisdom and power of the world into foolishness and gives us another kind of wisdom and power. Because it is his way to look into the depths and to see what is despised, I have translated the word *humilitas* as "nothing" or "lowly creature," so that Mary's meaning here is: "God has regarded me, a poor, despised, lowly girl, though he could have found a rich, famous, noble, mighty queen, or the daughter of a prince or a lord. He could have found the daughter of Annas or of Caiaphas, men who held the highest position in the land, but instead he cast his pure and gracious eyes on me and used a lowly, despised maiden so that no one would boast that they were worthy of it. And I must also acknowledge that this is all due to pure grace and goodness and not my own merit or worthiness."

Luther's *Commentary on the Magnificat*

We have said enough above about the tender Virgin's lowly being and status and how completely unexpected was the honor that God so graciously bestowed upon her. Thus she does not revel in her worthiness or unworthiness, but only in the divine regard, which is so exceedingly good and gracious that God would look upon such a lowly maiden in such a glorious and honorable way. People do her an injustice when they say that she did not glory in her virginity, but rather in her humility. She did not extol either, but gloried only in God's gracious regard. Accordingly, the emphasis here is not on the word *humilitatem* (lowliness) but on the word *respexit* (he regards), for her lowliness is not to be praised, but rather God's regard of her is to be praised. This is similar to when a prince reaches out his hand to a poor beggar; it is not the beggar's lowliness that is laudable, but the prince's grace and goodness.

In order to dispel such false illusions and to distinguish the correct from false humility, we will digress a moment and take a look at humility, with respect to which many have erred. "Humility" in German is what Paul terms in Greek and Latin *affectus vilitatis seu sensus humilium rerum*: a love and tendency toward lowly and despised things. Now, we know many people who bring water to the fountain (that is, who go out with humble clothing, people, gestures, places, and words), but only with the intention to be seen by the powerful, wealthy, learned, and saints as good, and as the kind of people who deign to consort with lowly things. For if they knew that no one cared about what they do, they would be at a loss because theirs is an artificial humility. Their cunning eye only looks at the reward and the success of their humility, not on the lowly thing itself without any concern for reward or success. Their humility ceases when there is no longer any promise of reward or success. One may not describe such people as having the will or heart for lowly things, but they have only their thoughts, lips, hands, clothes, and the outward appearance of it. Meanwhile, their heart looks to higher, greater things, which they hope to achieve through the appearance of humility, yet these people believe themselves to be humble, saintly people.

The truly humble do not look at the results of their humility, but with simple hearts look upon the lowly, associate with them, and are themselves never aware that they are humble. Here the water flows from the source; it follows naturally and as a matter of course that they will cultivate lowly conduct, words, places, persons, and clothing, and will avoid, wherever possible, high and mighty things. As King David says in Psalm 131:1: "My heart is not proud, O Lord, my eyes are not haughty; I do not concern myself with great matters or things too wonderful for me." And Job 22:29: "When people are brought low and you say, 'it is pride'; then he will save the downcast." Therefore honor comes to them unexpectedly, and they are elevated without knowing it, because they were simply satisfied with their lowly station and not concerned with elevation. But the falsely humble wonder why their honor and elevation are delayed and their secret, false pride is not satisfied with their lowly station, but they secretly aspire to ever greater heights.

Thus, true humility, as I have already said, never knows it is humble, for if it knew that, it would become haughty from contemplating such a wonderful virtue. Rather, the humble cling with heart, will, and all their senses to the lowly things; they keep them continually in their sights and carry these images around with them. And because they have the lowly continually in their sights, they cannot see anything else nor can they be aware of themselves, even less of lofty things, so any honor and elevation comes as a surprise and finds itself in line with a mind that has no time for honor or elevation. Thus Luke 1:29 says that Mary found the angel's greeting astonishing and she wondered at what kind of greeting this was that she never could have foreseen. If the greeting had come to Caiaphas' daughter, on the other hand, she would not have wondered at the greeting, but would have received it immediately and thought: "Well, this is appropriate and a good thing."

On the other hand, false humility is not aware when it is proud, for if it knew that, it would soon be humiliated due to a reputation for lack of virtue, but it clings with heart, mind, and sense to lofty things, which it has unceasingly before its eyes. These are the images that it thinks about continually, and since it does so, it cannot see itself or be aware of itself. Thus honors do not come to it without forethought or anticipation, since it is already full of these thoughts, but shame and dishonor take it by surprise because it is preoccupied with entirely different thoughts.

It does not do any good to try to teach the wise humility by regarding lowly, despised things. And by the same token, no one becomes proud by regarding lofty things. It is not the images themselves, but the way of seeing that has to change. We have to spend our lives here among lofty and lowly images, and as Christ says (Matthew 5:29; 18:9), the eye must be plucked out. Moses does not say (Genesis 3:7) that after the fall Adam and Eve focused on different things than before, but he says that their eyes were opened so that they realized they were naked, even though they had been naked before but were not aware of it. Queen Esther wore an expensive crown, yet she said it seemed but a filthy rag in her eyes (Esther 14:16, Apocrypha[6]). Lofty things were not removed from her sight, but being a mighty queen, she had them in great abundance. There was not one lowly thing within her sight, yet her eyes were humble. Her heart and mind did not pay attention to lofty things; thus God accomplished amazing things through her. Therefore, it is not the things, but we who must be changed in heart and mind, because then we will learn to spurn and avoid lofty things and to heed and seek after lowly things. In this case, humility is good in every way and is steadfast, yet never aware of its own humility. This leads to joy and the heart remains steadfast and whole whether things change or remain, are high or low, great or small.

Oh, there is much hidden pride behind the humble clothing, speech, and demeanor that fills today's world. People despise themselves so that others will not; they flee from honors so that honors will pursue them; they avoid lofty things so that they will nevertheless be praised and their lowly things not regarded as being too low. But here the young Virgin points to nothing but her lowly estate, in which she gladly had lived and would have remained. She never thought about honors or lofty things and was never conscious of her own humility. For humility is so noble and precious that it cannot tolerate introspection, but is only subject to God's gaze, as it says in Psalm 113:6: "He looks far down upon the lowly in the heavens and the earth." For whoever is cognizant of one's own humility would also be in a position to judge one's own humility and thus preempt God's judgment, even though we know that God's judgment makes one blessed. That is why the right must be reserved for God himself to know and to see humility and to hide it among the lowly things with such provision and practice that we even forget to look at ourselves. That is the purpose of suffering, death, and all kinds of adversity on earth, in order to shape us and help us, as a result of cares and toil, to let go of false perspectives.

Now it is clear from the word *humilitatem* that the Virgin Mary was a poor, lowly, insignificant girl who served God and did not know that her lowly station would be so highly prized by God. This is to comfort us so that though we might be willingly humbled and scorned, we should not give up,

---

6. *Apocrypha* is a Greek word meaning "hidden." It refers to books between the Old and New Testaments. Some books are canonical to the Roman Catholic and Eastern Orthodox Churches. Some are canonical to the Eastern Orthodox Church but not the Roman Catholic Church. None are canonical for the Lutheran Church.

as though God is angry with us, but rather it should give us hope that he is merciful. Only thus will we be concerned that we are not sufficiently satisfied and content in our low estate, and that our corrupt eyes are perhaps too open and wide, betraying us with a secret desire for lofty things or satisfaction with ourselves, and thus bringing all humility to naught. For what advantage is it to the damned to be brought to a low condition and then not be satisfied with their lot? And what harm does it do to the angels to be elevated to the heights, as long as they do not cling to it with false desire? In short, this verse teaches us to know God correctly because it shows that God regards the lowly and despised. For one knows God correctly when one knows that God sees and recognizes the lowly, as said above, and from this knowledge flows love and trust in God, so that one gladly yields to him and willingly follows him.

As Jeremiah says (Jeremiah 9:23, 24): "Do not let the wise boast in their wisdom, do not let the mighty boast in their might, do not let the wealthy boast in their wealth; but let those who boast boast in this, that they understand and know me." And St. Paul teaches (2 Corinthians 10:17): "'Let the one who boasts, boast in the Lord.'" After the Mother of God praises her God and Savior with a simple, pure spirit and does not presume to deserve his gifts, thus having rightly sung of his goodness, she next praises his goodness and his works. For, as said above, we must not cling to God's gifts and grasp after them, but press on through them, clinging only to him and his goodness. Only then can one also praise him in his works, in which he has shown us such goodness (love, trust, and praise), so that works are nothing other than the occasion to love and praise his pure goodness, which reigns over us.

Mary begins with herself and sings about what he has done for her, teaching us a two-part lesson. First, she teaches us that we should pay attention to what God does for us and not concentrate on what he does for others, for you will not be saved by what God does for other people, but by what he does for you. As it says in the last chapter of the Gospel of John (21:21): "[Peter asked,] 'Lord, what about him [John]?'" Christ answered by saying (21:22): "'what is that to you? Follow me.'" It is as if he wanted to say: "John's works will not help you. You must take your turn and wait for what I will do for you." Nevertheless, these days the world is captive to terrible abuses in which good works are apportioned out and sold, where several presumptuous spirits have seen fit to help those whom they presume would live or die without them, as if they themselves had a surplus of such good works, even though Paul says plainly in 1 Corinthians 3:8: "Each will receive wages according to the labor of each"—certainly not for the labors of another.

It would be all right if they prayed for other people or brought their works before God as an intercession, but they treat them as if they were their own works to give away, which is scandalous. And the worst of it is that they give away their works without really knowing the value God places on them because God does not see the works, but the heart and faith by means of which he works in us. They do not pay any attention to this, but only to their own external works, deceiving themselves and everyone else. It has gone so far that they persuade men to wear a monk's cowl as they are dying, as if, dying in such holy garb, the person might receive indulgences from sin and be saved, thus saving people not just by the works of another but by means of someone else's clothes.

In fact, if one does not watch out, the evil spirit will go so far as to send people to heaven by means of monastic diet, cells, and burial. (Good grief, what great darkness is this? A monk's cowl makes a man pious and saves him!) So, what use is faith then? Let us all become monks and die in a monk's frock! In this way, all the cloth would go to make monks cowls! Watch out and beware of wolves in sheep's clothing; they will deceive you and tear you to pieces. Remember that God is at work in you and that your salvation is based only on what God does in you and no one else, as you see exemplified here in the Virgin Mary. When you allow other people to intercede for you, that is right and proper, because we should pray for one another and help each other. But no one should rely on another's works and ignore the divine works done in them. Rather, they should recognize what God has done for them with all due diligence and not bother about others, behaving as if only God and they were in heaven and earth, and God had no one else to look after. And only then can they look at the works of others.

The other thing that Mary teaches is that everyone should first want to praise God and extol his works on their behalf and then praise God for what he does for others. Thus we read (in Acts 15:12) that Paul and Barnabas relayed to the apostles the works of God done through them, and likewise the apostles relayed the same about themselves. They did the same thing after the appearance of the resurrected Christ (Luke 24:34–35). And there arose a common jubilation and praise of God, with each person praising God's grace for the other, but most of all because of the grace he/she received, although it might be less than what another person received.

They were zealous not about being the first or foremost in terms of gifts, but rather in praising and loving God. They were so simple-minded that God and his pure goodness were enough, no matter how small the gifts. But the egotists and self-absorbed became suspicious and confused when they become aware that they are not the recipients of the highest and best gifts in relation to others. They grumble rather than praise when they find out that they are the same or lower than the lowly, as in the Gospel of Matthew 20:11–16, where the laborers grumbled against the master of the house not because he cheated them, but because he paid everyone the same wages.

Therefore, today we still find many who do not praise God's goodness because they do not see that they have as much as St. Peter or some other saint or as this one or that one on earth. They think that if only they had that much, they too would also praise and love God. They hardly notice that they are overflowing with God's goodness, which they do not recognize, in terms of body, life, reason, goods, honor, friends, and the energy of the sun, like all other creatures. Even if they had all the gifts given to Mary, these people would not recognize God in them or praise him; for as Christ says in Luke 16:10: "Whoever is faithful in a very little is faithful also in much; and whoever is dishonest in a very little is dishonest also in much." Therefore, they do not deserve abundance or greatness because they spurn the small and insignificant. But if they praised God in the small things, they would receive an abundance of great things. They act as they do because they look up and not down. If they looked down, they would find many people who do not have half of what they have, yet are happy with God and praise him. A bird sings and is happy because of what it can do, and does not grumble because it cannot speak. A dog jumps joyfully about and is content though it does not possess the gift of reason. All animals are content as they are and serve God with love and praise. Only the evil, selfish eye of a person, which is insatiable and is never satisfied due to its ingratitude and pride, always wants the highest seat of honor (Luke 14:8) and is not willing to honor God, but wants to be honored by God. Thus we read that during the time of the Council of Constance, two cardinals were riding in a field when they saw a shepherd standing and crying. The one cardinal, a good person, did not want to pass by, but stopped to comfort the man. He rode up to him and asked him what the matter was. The shepherd started to cry even more and for the longest time could not say anything, so that the cardinal became quite concerned. Finally, the shepherd recovered himself and pointed to a frog saying: "I'm crying because God has fashioned me so

Luther's *Commentary on the Magnificat*

wonderfully and not ugly like this reptile, but I have never acknowledged it, thanked or praised him for it." The cardinal beat his breast and was so shocked by these words that he fell from his mount and had to be carried away. He cried: "O Saint Augustine, how right you were that the unlearned rise and enter heaven before us, while we with our learning walk around in flesh and blood." I am sure that the shepherd was neither rich, nor handsome, nor powerful, but nevertheless had reflected on God's goodness so deeply and thankfully that he found more in them than he himself was able to comprehend.

Mary confesses that the main work that God did in her was to regard her, which is indeed the greatest of his works upon which all the others depend and from which they flow. For where it happens that God turns his eyes on someone and notices that person, there is grace and blessedness, and all manner of gifts and works follow. Thus we read in Genesis 4:4–5 that God saw Abel and his offering, but he did not notice Cain and his. Also, the majority of prayers in the Psalms talk about God turning his face toward us, not hiding it from us, making his face shine upon us, and so on. The fact that Mary regards this as the most important thing is indicated where she says (Luke 1:48): "Behold, since he has regarded me, all generations will call me blessed."

Notice the words: she does not say one will say all kinds of good things about her, will praise her virtue, her virginity or humility, or sing a little song about what she has done, but only because of this one thing, that God has regarded her, will people call her blessed. That is, in its purest form, giving God alone the glory. She points to God's regard for her and says: "Look, from now on all generations will call me blessed." In other words, from that point in time when God regarded my lowliness, people will call me blessed. Thus, it is not she who is praised, but God's grace to her is praised. In fact, she is despised and despises herself when she points out that God has regarded her lowly condition. Therefore she first lauds her blessedness before telling about the works that God has done on her behalf, attributing them all to the fact that God regarded her lowly condition.

From this we can learn how to show her the honor and devotion that are due her. How should one address her? Consider these words and they will teach you to say: "Oh blessed Virgin, Mother of God, you were nothing, lowly and despised, yet God has so richly regarded you in his grace and done great things in you. You were not worthy of any of them, but the rich, lavish love of God's grace was upon you, through no merit of your own. Hail to you! Blessed are you from this hour forth and to eternity for discovering such a God." You do not need to fear that she will be upset if you find her unworthy of such grace. For she undoubtedly did not lie when she confessed that she was unworthy and nothing, someone whom God regarded out of his pure grace and not because of any merit of her own.

She does not like to listen to the vain chatterboxes who proclaim and write about her merits. They just want to show off their own great artistic skill and do not see how they oppress the Magnificat, make the Mother of God out to be a liar, and diminish the grace of God. For to the degree we attribute merit and worthiness to her, to that extent we also devalue the grace of God and diminish the truth of the Magnificat. Also, the angel greets her only as the "highly favored of God" (Luke 1:28) because the Lord is with her, which is why she is blessed among women. Therefore all those who heap such praise and honor upon her and who attribute everything to her are in danger of making her into an idol, as if it were her own doing that people should honor her and look to her for good things, though she points away from herself so that God will be honored in her and that through her everyone will have confidence in God's grace.

Therefore, whoever wants to honor her properly must not regard her as alone and by herself, but as in the presence of God and far beneath him, and consider her in her nothingness in that place (as she said). Then one must marvel at the abundant grace of God who mercifully regards, embraces, and richly blesses such a lowly and despised mortal. Seeing her in this way, one will be moved to love God and praise him for his grace, and thus will be motivated to look to such a God for all good things, who looks graciously upon the poor, despised, and lowly, and does not reject them, so that their hearts are strengthened in faith, love, and hope. Do you not think that she would like nothing better than if you were to come to God through her in this way and from her learn to trust and hope in God, even though you are despised and nothing, whether in life or in death? She does not want you to come to her, but to come to God through her.

By the same token, you should learn to fear all lofty things that people strive after when you see that even for his mother God did not seek or desire a prestigious person. The artists who portray and paint our Holy Virgin as someone who is not despised, but rather great and lofty, effectively comparing her with us rather than with God, make us timid and afraid and hide her comforting image, as they do during Lent. For there is no example by which we can be comforted, because they elevate her above all others as the highest example of God's grace. But she would rather encourage all the world to be confident in God's grace, to praise and love it, so that all hearts would win such an opinion of God through her and could say with confidence: "Oh Blessed Virgin, Mother of God, God has shown us such great comfort in you because he regarded you despite your unworthiness and lowliness. From now on we should therefore be reminded that he will also regard us poor, lowly creatures just as he did you."

Do you not think that if David, Peter, Paul, Mary Magdalene, and others like them are given as examples of unworthiness of God's great grace in order to give us comfort and to strengthen our confidence in God and our faith, that the blessed Mother of God would also gladly want to be such an example to all the world? But she cannot be this because of the abundant eulogists and chatterboxes who from this verse do not reveal how in her the effusive riches of God joined with her deep poverty, divine honor with her lowly condition, divine glory with her contemptibility, divine greatness with her smallness, divine goodness with her lack of merit, and divine grace with her unworthiness, so that love and affection toward God would grow with all assurance, which is why all of her deeds, as well as the lives and deeds of all the saints, have been recorded. And now we have many people who come to her for help and comfort as if she were a god, so that I am concerned that there is now more idolatry in the world than ever before. But enough of that for now.

I have translated the Latin phrase *omnes generationes* in the German as "children's children," though it really means "all generations." The expression is obscure because many have tried very hard to understand how it is possible that all generations should call her blessed when Jews, heathens, and many bad Christians malign her or, at the very least, treat her with contempt. They think that they understand the word "generations" as the whole of humankind, but here it means the familial line of descent from father to son, grandson, and so on. Every member is called a generation, so that the Virgin Mary means nothing else than this: her praise will be sung from one generation to another so that there will be no period of time in which she will not be praised. She shows this when she says: "See, henceforth all generations," meaning it begins now and will continue throughout all generations, to children's children.

The word *makariusi* (Greek) means more than to simply "call blessed"; it means to "bless," or "make blessed." This blessedness does not happen with mere words or sayings, with kneeling, bowing, taking off one's hat, making images, building churches, which even the wicked can do, but it is done with all of one's strength and utmost sincerity. This happens when the heart (as said above) is moved by observing her lowly condition and God's grace combined, and as a result is joyful and happy because of her example and can say or think it wholeheartedly: "O Blessed Virgin Mary!" Such blessedness is very appropriately due her, as we have heard.

IV. For the Mighty One has done great things for me, and holy is his name (v. 49).

Here Mary sings of all of the works that God has done for her and lists them in order. In the previous verse she sang about God's regard and gracious will toward her, which, as we have said, is the greatest and main work of grace. Here she sings of works and gifts, for God gives good things to many people and generously adorns them, as he did Lucifer in heaven. He showers his gifts upon the masses, but he nevertheless does not regard them. His good things are only gifts that last for a season, but his grace and regard are an inheritance that is eternal, as Paul says in Romans 6:23: "The free gift of God is eternal life." In giving us gifts, he gives us what he has, but in giving us his regard and grace, he gives us himself. In his gifts, we receive his hand, but in his gracious regard we receive his heart, spirit, mind, and will. Thus the Blessed Virgin gives his regard the highest and first place and does not say at the start: "All generations will call me blessed because he has done great things for me," as this verse says, but she says, as in the preceding verse: "He has regarded my lowliness and low estate." Where there is God's gracious will, there are also his gifts, but the opposite is not the case (namely, that where his gifts are, there is also his gracious will). That is why this verse correctly follows the previous one. So we read in Genesis 25:5–6 that Abraham gave gifts to the children of his concubines, but to Isaac, his legitimate son by his legitimate wife Sarah, he gave the entire inheritance. Therefore, God does not want his legitimate children to put their trust in good things or gifts, spiritual or temporal, however great and many they may be, but they are to put their trust in his grace and in him, yet without disparaging his gifts.

Mary does not enumerate God's gifts specifically, but includes them all together in one word and says: "He has done great things for me"; in other words: "Everything he has done for me is great." Here she teaches us that the greater the heart's devotion, the less there is need for words, for she feels

Luther's *Commentary on the Magnificat*

that she cannot adequately express in words what she thinks. Therefore, these few words of the spirit are so great and so deep that no one can understand them unless they too have the same spirit, at least in part. But for the non-spiritual, who deal in many words and make a lot of noise, such words seem too insignificant and entirely without flavor. Christ also teaches in Matthew 6:7 that we should not be verbose when we pray, for that is what unbelievers do because they think they will be heard on account of their many words. Even today in churches there is a lot of bell ringing, piping, singing, shouting, and intoning, but I fear precious little praise of God, who wants to be worshiped in spirit and in truth, as it says in John 4:24.

In Proverbs 27:14, Solomon says: "Whoever blesses a neighbor with a loud voice, rising early in the morning, will be counted as cursing." For this kind of person arouses suspicion by making everyone think the person is whitewashing something bad, by protesting so much the person makes everything worse. Conversely, whoever maligns a neighbor with a loud voice and gets up early to do it (in other words, is not lazy but very vigorous about it) is considered to be praising the neighbor. For people then think that it is not true, but that what the person says is out of hatred and malice, which only serves to make the person look worse and the neighbor look better. And when people think to worship God with a loud voice, with many words, sounds, and noise, they behave as if he were either deaf or ignorant, as if we should have to wake him up or instruct him. Such an opinion of God works more to his disgrace and dishonor than to his praise. But those who consider his divine deeds in the depths of their hearts and regard them with wonder and thanks, so that they break forth with fervent emotion, express praise more in sighs than in words. The words flow forth without any forethought so that the spirit streams out with them and the words live; they have hands and feet. Indeed, the whole body and all of life and limb desire to speak. That is true praise of God in spirit and in truth, where the words are all fire, light, and life, as David says in Psalm 119:140: "Your promise is well tried," and again in Psalm 119:171: "My lips will pour forth praise," like boiling water overflows and steam pours out because the pot cannot contain the heat any longer. These are the kinds of words sung by the Virgin in this hymn, and though few, they are profound and great. In Romans 12:11, St. Paul calls such people "ardent in spirit" and teaches us to be likewise.

The "great things" are nothing other than this: she became the Mother of God, by which so many great and good things were given to her that they are beyond human understanding. For from this flows all honor and blessing and her peerless place among all of humankind, since there is no one like her because she had a child by our heavenly Father, and such a child. And she herself cannot give a name to the overwhelming greatness of the work and must let it be what it is, so that she is overwhelmed by the fact that there are such great things beyond words or measure. Therefore, people have compiled all of her honor in one phrase by calling her "Mother of God." No one can say anything greater about her, though he had as many tongues as leaves on a tree, grass, stars in heaven, or the sand in the sea. We should profoundly reflect on what it means to be the Mother of God.

Mary also attributes everything to God's grace and not to her own merit, for though she is free of sin, this grace is so extraordinary that she would not deserve it under any circumstances. How could any creature be worthy of being the Mother of God? And although there are numerous scribes who like to go on about her worthiness of such motherhood, I believe her more than I do them. She says that God regarded her nothingness and did not reward her according to merit, but rather "has done great things for me." He has done this all on his own, without her deserving anything. In her entire life would she have thought to become the Mother of God, even less be prepared for it or capable of it? Luke writes that this message took her totally by surprise (Luke 1:29). Merit, however, is not unprepared for reward, but is always ready and willing to accept a reward.

The fact the text of the (Easter) hymn says: "Joy to Thee, O Queen of Heaven . . . you have earned," and in another place: "You were worthy to bear," proves nothing, since we sing the same words about the Holy Cross that was made of wood and cannot earn anything. The text should be understood in this way: to be the Mother of God, she had to be a woman and a virgin from the tribe of Judah and must believe the angel's message in order to be worthy of it, as was written in the Scriptures. Just as that piece of wood had no merit or worthiness other than that it was suitable for a cross and was used by God for that purpose, so Mary's worthiness for this kind of motherhood consisted in nothing else than that she was suited for it and appointed to it. This was to show that it was out of pure grace and not a reward, so that nothing would be taken away from God's grace, worship, and honor by giving her too much credit, for it is better to take away from her worthiness than to take away from God's grace. Indeed, one cannot take too much away from her since she was created out of nothing like all other creatures. It may be easy for us to greatly diminish God's grace, but it is a dangerous thing to do and not at all pleasing to her. There should be limits to extolling her name, such as that of "Queen of Heaven," even though it is true. Nevertheless, she is not a goddess and cannot give aid or help, as the pious think when they pray to her and flee to her more than to God. She can give nothing, but only God can, as we shall see next.

With these words, "for the Mighty One," she takes away all might and power from all other creatures and gives them only to God. What great boldness and theft from such a young, small girl! With these words she makes all the strong infirm, all the mighty weak, all the wise foolish, all the famous despised, and attributes only to God power, deeds, wisdom, and glory. The phrase "the Mighty One" is the same as saying that no one does anything on their own, but as Paul says in Ephesians 1:11: God "accomplishes all things," and all creatures' works are God's works. As we confess in the Creed: "I believe in God the Father Almighty." He is almighty because it is only his power that works in all, through all, and above all. Thus Samuel's mother Hannah sings in 1 Samuel 2:9: "for not by might does one prevail." And St. Paul says in 2 Corinthians 3:5: "Not that we are competent of ourselves to claim anything as coming from us; our competence is from God." This is an important text and incorporates many things. It puts down all pride, arrogance, sacrilege, fame, and false confidence and exalts God alone. It shows why God alone is to be exalted, namely, that he does all things. This is easy to say, but hard to believe and to translate into life. Those who practice it are the most peace-loving, serene, simple people who do not claim anything for themselves but know that it is God alone who is at work.

This, then, is the meaning of the words of the Mother of God: "It is not me in all of these great and good things, but only he who does all things and whose power is at work in all things and who has done great things for me." Here the word "might" does not mean some kind of latent power—the way one uses it, for example, to refer to a king even when he sits still and does not do anything—but rather means an active power and constant activity that is continually engaged, moving, and acting. God never rests, but is always at work, as Christ says in John 5:17: "My Father is still working, and I also am working." Similarly, Paul says in Ephesians 3:20: "to him who . . . is able to accomplish abundantly far more than all we can ask or imagine"; that is, he always does more than we ask because that is his way and how his power works. That is why I have said that Mary does not want to be an idol. She does nothing; God does all. We ought to call upon her so that God will give and do what we ask for her sake. We should call on all of the other saints in the same way, so that the work remains totally God's alone.

Therefore she adds: "and holy is his name." That is: "Just as I do not make any claim to the work, I likewise do not make any claim to the name and the honor. For the person who does the work deserves the honor and the name. It is unfair that one person should do the work while another receives the name and thus the glory. I am only the workshop that he used, but I have contributed nothing to the work itself. No one should praise me or give me honor for becoming the Mother of God, but God and his work are to be honored and praised in me. It is enough that one rejoices with me and calls me blessed because God used me to do such a great work in me." See how purely she traces everything back to God and attributes absolutely no work, honor, or glory to herself? She behaves no differently than before when she had nothing and asks for no more honor than before. She does not puff herself up or elevate herself and does not go out of her way to tell how she became the Mother of God. She does not demand any honor, but goes around and about the house as before, milking the cows, cooking, washing the dishes, sweeping, doing what any typical housemaid or matron does in the way of humble and despised tasks as if such overwhelming goodness and grace were not evident. She was regarded no more highly than the other neighbors and women than she was before and did not ask to be, but remained a humble maiden like many others. Oh, what a simple and pure heart she had and what a marvelous child she was! What great things lay hidden under such a humble exterior! How many people came into contact with her, spoke to her, ate and drank with her, yet likely regarded her as nothing more than a common, poor, humble girl but who would have fled from her in terror had they known the truth about her? That is the meaning of "and holy is his name," for "holy" means set apart and dedicated to God, something that no one should touch or defile, but rather should hold in honor. And "name" means a good reputation, fame, praise, and honor. Thus, everyone should leave God's name alone, not infringe on it or appropriate it for themselves. We get a picture of this in Exodus 30:25–32 when, at God's command, Moses made a special holy ointment and was strictly forbidden to allow anyone to use it on his skin. This means that no one should attribute God's name to oneself. We desecrate God's name when we allow ourselves to be honored or praised, or when we are pleased with ourselves or congratulate ourselves for our deeds and possessions as the world does, thus dishonoring and desecrating the name of God. But just as the works are God's alone, so too should the name belong to him alone. And all who thus hallow his name, denying any honor or glory to themselves, rightly honor his name and are therefore hallowed by it. As it says in Exodus 30:29, the ointment was so holy that it hallowed whatever it touched. In the same way, God's name is rightly honored by us when we hallow it by claiming no work, honor, or self-satisfaction of our own, but thus in turn it touches us and hallows us.

Therefore we must be vigilant because we cannot live on this earth without God's goodness and therefore also cannot live without his good name and honor. Therefore if someone praises us and we receive a good name because of it, we should take the example of the Mother of God and be ready to respond in the words of this verse, thus accepting correctly the honor and praise. We should say publicly, or at least think in our heart: "O Lord God, it is your work that is being praised and honored. Praised be your name. Not I, but you, O Lord, who does all things, have done this. Holy is your name." One should not negate praise and honor as if they were not valued, nor should one disparage them as if they were of no value, but rather not accept them as having more weight than they should, but give God in heaven the credit, to whom they rightly belong. That is what this noble verse teaches. It also answers the question whether one person ought to praise another. Indeed, St. Paul says in Romans 12:10 that we should "outdo one another in showing honor." But no one should accept the honor as if they have deserved it or internalize it too much, but should hallow it and ascribe it to God to whom it belongs, along with all other good things and good works that bring about honor. For no one should live a life without honor. If one would live an honorable life, then there must be honor. However, just as an honorable life is a gift and work of God, so too is the name alone his, holy and untouched by self-congratulation. This is what we pray in the Lord's Prayer: "Hallowed be thy name."

V. His mercy is for those who fear him from generation to generation (v. 50).

We must get used to the way Scripture uses the word "generation" to mean the natural succession of birth, in which one person is descended from another, as stated above. That is why the German word *Geschlecht* (generation) is not adequate, though I do not know of a better term, since by the term *generations* we (Germans) mean family or the bond of blood relations.

But here the word means the natural succession from father to son and grandson, with each member being called a generation, so that I think that the following would not be a bad translation: "And his mercy endures to the children's children of those who fear him." This is a common expression in the Scriptures and has its origin in the words God spoke to Moses and all the people on Mount Sinai in the words of the First Commandment (Exodus 20:5–6), saying: "I the Lord your God am a jealous God, punishing children for the iniquity of parents, to the third and the fourth generation of those who reject me, but showing steadfast love to the thousandth generation of those who love me and keep my commandments."

Now that she has sung about herself and God's goodness to her and has sung God's praises, Mary walks us through the works that God does for all people and praises them, teaching us to understand the works, ways, nature, and will of God. There are many highly intelligent people and philosophers who have earnestly tried to discover the nature of God. They have written much about him, each saying something different, but all have been blinded in the process and lacked the proper insight. It is indeed the greatest thing in heaven and on earth that one should know God correctly, even if one were to know only in part. Here the Mother of God does a good job of teaching anyone who wants to understand, just as she learned it for herself as seen above. How can one understand God any better than through his own works? Whoever rightly understands his works cannot fail to understand his nature, will, heart, and mind. That is why to understand his works is an art. And so that we can understand it more clearly, in the next four verses Mary enumerates six divine works in as many people, dividing the world into two parts with three works per person, positioning each over against its counterpart, thus showing what God does for both sides, portraying him so well that it could not be done any better.

This division is good and well-conceived and based on other places in Scripture, such as in Jeremiah 9:23–24, where it says: "Do not let the wise boast in their wisdom, do not let the mighty boast in their might, do not let the wealthy boast in their wealth; but let those who boast boast in this, that they understand and know me, that I am the Lord; I act with steadfast love, justice, and righteousness in the earth, for in these things I delight, says the Lord." This is a righteous text and corresponds to the hymn sung by the Mother of God. Here we see also that God divides everything in the world into three parts, wisdom, power, and wealth, and that everything they touch breaks, so he says that no one should put any store in them, for no one will find him in them nor does he take any pleasure in them. Over against these he posits three others: kindness, justice, and righteousness. "I am to be found in these things," he says: "I am so near that I do not work in heaven, but on earth is where you can find me. And whoever understands me may take comfort in and rely on that. For if one is not wise, but is poor in spirit, my mercy is with the person; if one is not powerful, but oppressed, my justice is there and will save the person; if one is not rich, but rather is poor and needy, the more the person has of my righteousness."

Under the word "wisdom" he includes spiritual gifts and excellence, by which a person gains popularity, fame, and a good reputation, as the next verse will show. Gifts such as intellect, reason, wit, skill, piety, virtue, a good life—in short, everything about the soul that people call divine and spiritual—all great and excellent gifts, yet none of them are God. Under the word "power" he includes all authority, nobility, friends, status, and honor, whether regarding temporal or spiritual goods and people (though in the Scriptures there is no spiritual authority or power, but only servants and subjects) together with all of the rights, freedom, and privileges that go along with them. Under "riches" are included health, beauty, pleasure, strength, and everything that helps a person's external looks. In opposition to these are three others: the poor in spirit, the oppressed, and those who lack the necessities of life. Now we will take a look at these six works in order.

The First Work of God: Mercy

This verse says of mercy: "His mercy is for those who fear him from generation to generation." Mary begins with the highest and greatest things, that is, with the spiritual and internal things that make for the most arrogant, proud, and stubborn people on earth. There is no rich or mighty lord nearly so puffed up and bold as the know-it-all who feels and thinks that he is right, best understands the issue, and is wiser than everyone else. Especially in a situation where such people must yield or are in the wrong, they become so defiant and entirely lacking in the fear of God that they dare to boast that they are not wrong, that God is on their side, and that everyone else is of the devil. They dare to appeal to the judgment of God, and when given the opportunity and power, they rush headlong, pursuing, condemning, maligning, silencing, banishing, and destroying all who disagree with them, saying afterward that they did it to serve and honor God. They are more certain of receiving thanks and reward from God than are the angels in heaven! Oh what great gas-bags they are! The Scripture has much to say about such people and threatens them with many dreadful things, but they feel it even less than an anvil feels a blacksmith's hammer. This is a large, widespread phenomenon.

Christ says of such people in John 16:2: "Indeed, an hour is coming when those who kill you will think that by doing so they are offering worship to God." And in Psalm 10:5–6 it says of the same crowd: "As for their foes, they scoff at them. They think in their hearts, 'We shall not . . . meet adversity,'" as if to say: "I am right, I do good things, and God will richly reward me as a result." The Moabites[7] were such a people, as it says in Isaiah 16:6 and Jeremiah 48:29–30: "We have heard of the pride of Moab—he is very proud—of his loftiness, his pride, and his arrogance. . . ." His reputation and his wrath were greater than his power. Thus, we see that such people would gladly do more as a result of their arrogance than they are really able to do, like the Jews were in their dealings with Christ and the apostles. Such types were the friends of Job, who argued against him with excessive wisdom, praising and preaching God in lofty terms. Such people do not listen and you cannot tell them anything because it is impossible for them to be wrong or to concede. They maintain their position though the world should go to ruin! The Scriptures cannot punish such a lost crowd enough. Here it calls them snakes with plugged ears so they cannot hear; here an untamable wild ox; now a raging lion; and here a great, immovable boulder; a dragon, etc. (Psalm 58:5; Psalm 22:21–22; Psalm 7:2; Jeremiah 5:3; Psalm 74:13).

Nowhere are these people more aptly portrayed than in Job 40:10–24 and 41:1–11, where he calls them the Behemoth. A Behemah is a single beast, but a Behemoth is a herd of beasts, or a crowd of people who have a beastly mind and will not allow the Spirit of God to rule in them. God describes them as having eyes like the "eyelids of the dawn" (41:18), for their cleverness is without limits. Its hide is so hard that it laughs at the arrow and the javelin (41:28–29), meaning that when they are contradicted, they laugh in scorn because their correctness should not be questioned. "Its back is made of shields in rows, shut up closely as with a seal. One is so near to another that no air can come between them" (41:15–16). "Its heart," says God, "is as hard as stone" (41:24). It is the body of the devil, which is why he ascribes the same things to the devil in this passage. In our times such

---

7. The Moabites lived on the east side of the Dead Sea.

people are clearly the pope and his crowd and have been for a long time. They do all of these things and more. They do not listen and they do not relent. It does not help to talk, to give advice, to beg, or threaten. Nothing helps. In short, they are right and that is all there is to it, in spite of everyone, though it be the whole world.

But if someone were to say: "How can that happen? Should we not defend what is right? Should we let the truth go? Did not the holy martyrs die for the sake of the Gospel? Did not Christ himself claim to be right? Of course, it is the case that such people can be right publicly (and as they whine, before God) and act wisely and well," my answer is that now is the right time to open your eyes because herein lies the crux of the matter: everything depends on the meaning of "being in the right." It is true that we should suffer all things because of truth and right, and not disavow it, however insignificant the instance. It may also be the case that sometimes these people are right, but they spoil it by not treating it correctly with fear or by not looking to God, but think that it is enough that they are right and should and will keep going on their own power. They keep up the game, but in so doing they make their right into a wrong, even if they were basically right. Even more dangerous is the case when they only think they are right, but are not sure, as in the case of lofty things pertaining to God and his right. Let us first deal with the simpler issue of human achievement and start with an example that is easy to understand.

Is it not true that money, property, body, honor, wife, child, and friends are also good things created and given by God? Since they are God's gifts and not yours, what if he were to test you to see if you were willing to give them up for his sake, and to cling more to him than to such things? What if he sent an enemy who took all or part of it and did you harm? What if you lost them by death or accident? Do you think you would have just cause to rage and storm, try to take them back by force, or behave impatiently until they were returned to you? Do you profess that they were good things and God's creatures, made with his own hands, things all of Scriptures call good, which is why you would want to keep God's Word so that you can reclaim these good things and protect them with your body and life, or at least not do without them willingly, or let them go easily? Would that not be a sham as far as right is concerned? However, if you wanted to handle it correctly, you should not rush headlong, but should fear God and say: "Dear God, these are good things and your gifts, as your own word and Scriptures say. But I do not know if you will grant me them. If I knew that I should not have them, I would not move a hair to get them back. However, if I knew that you would rather that I have them than someone else, I will serve your will by retrieving them at the risk of my life and property. But since I do not know either way and see that for now you allow them to be taken from me, I leave the matter to you and will wait to see what I should do and be ready to have them or to do without them."

That is an example of a right soul that fears God, and there we see the mercy about which the Mother of God sings. Therefore, we can see why Abraham, David, and the people of Israel fought in ancient times and slew many. They went out into battle according to God's will and stood in fear and fought, not as a result of God's will, but because God commanded them to fight, as the biblical narratives generally portray God's other commands. And see how here the truth is not denied. The truth says that they are good things and God's creatures. But the same truth also says and teaches that you should let go of good things and be prepared at any moment to do without them, if God wills it, and to rely solely on God. The truth does not force you to take the things back, thus admitting that they are good. It also does not force you to say that they are not good, but rather to be inwardly free of them and to recognize that they are neither good nor bad.

We must treat justice and all manner of reason and wisdom the same way. Who doubts that justice is a good thing and a gift from God? God's Word itself says that the justice is good and that no one should admit that this good and just cause is unjust or bad; one should sooner die for it and let go of everything that is not God. For that would be to deny God and his Word, which says that justice is good and not evil. Would you not cry, rage, storm, and want to choke the entire world if justice is denied you or suppressed? Will you do as some people and cry to heaven, causing devastation for others, corrupting lands and people, filling the world with war and the spilling of blood? How do you know if God will let you keep such good things as well as your rights? It is his and he can take it from you today or tomorrow, outwardly or inwardly, by means of an enemy or a friend, as he wills. He tests you to see if you will give up your rights for his sake; if you will be wrong and suffer injustice for his sake, endure shame for his sake, and cling only to him. If you are now God-fearing and think: "Lord, it is yours. I will not keep it unless I know that you want me to have it. Whatever happens, you alone are my God," see, then, how true this verse is: "His mercy is on those who fear him," on those who refuse to do anything apart from his will. Here God's Word is kept in both aspects. In the first place, you confess that your rights, your reason, knowledge, wisdom, and all of your intentions are right and good, as God's Word declares. In the second place, you are willing to do without any of these things if it is God's will; to be wrongfully accused and the subject of shame before all the world, as God's Word also teaches.

It is one thing to confess what is right, and another to obtain what is right. If you have confessed what is good and right, that should be enough. Even if you cannot obtain it, God has been obeyed. You are commanded to confess and God has reserved the obtaining for himself. If he wills that you should obtain it, he will do it himself or put it in your way without you having to think about it, so that you must take it and will obtain it in a way that you never would have thought or expected (Ephesians 3:20). If not, be satisfied with his mercy (2 Corinthians 12:9). If they deprive you of the victory of your rights, they cannot take the confession away from you. Thus, we must not refrain from having God's good things, but from wickedly and perversely clinging to them so that with inner freedom we can either do without them or use them, and either way relying solely on God. Princes and rulers should know this so that they are satisfied with confessing justice and do not immediately try to gain it and then take it upon themselves, without the fear of God, to make the world a place of blood and suffering, thinking that they are doing something good and right because they have, or think they have, a just cause. This is no different than the proud and haughty people of Moab, who advance themselves and think that they deserve the fine, lovely goodness and gifts of God, though they are not worthy, if they were to see themselves in God's eyes, to walk the earth and eat crusts of bread because of their sins. O blindness, blindness! Who is worthy of God's smallest creature? Not only do we want to possess the highest creatures—the right, wisdom, and honor—but we want to keep and regain possession with fierce shedding of blood and all manner of disaster. We go around praying and fasting, going to Mass, and going to church with such a bloody, furious, and crazed demeanor that it is a wonder that the stones do not break apart in front of us.

Does this not beg the question? Should a ruler not defend his land and subjects against injustice, or keep still and allow everything to be taken? What would become of the world then? I will briefly give my opinion on the matter. Worldly power is responsible for protecting its citizens, as I have often said. For this reason it wields the sword in order to breed fear in those who do not heed such divine teaching, so that they will leave others alone and in peace. Additionally, temporal power does not seek its own ends in this, but rather the welfare of the neighbor and God's honor. It could have accomplished nothing and let the sword lie if God had not ordained things so as to control the wicked so that the act of protection does not do even greater harm, which is like being penny wise and pound foolish. It is poor protection when a ruler brings an entire city into danger to protect one person, or endangers the entire country for the sake of a village or a castle, unless God had specifically commanded it, as in earlier times. If a knight robs a citizen of his goods and the lord of the land sends an army to punish him, in the process destroying the land, who has done greater harm, the knight or the lord? King David looked the other way many times when he could not punish one without bringing harm to many others. All rulers must do the same. In turn, a citizen must be prepared to tolerate some discomfort for the sake of the majority and not desire that for the one citizen's sake the rest should be endangered. It will not always be thus. Christ does not want the weeds killed in case the wheat is killed in the process (Matthew 13:29). If people fought over every insult and did not overlook anything, we would never have peace and have nothing but pure depravity. Therefore, right or wrong is never a sufficient cause to indiscriminately punish or wage war. It is acceptable to punish within the limits of authority and without destroying another person. A lord or authority must always look at what benefits the majority rather than one single faction. The man of the house will never become rich if he tosses out the whole goose just because someone plucked a few feathers. But this is not the time to discuss the subject of war.

We must do the same in divine things, such as with faith and the Gospel, which are the highest goods and which one should never let go. However, accepting and retaining justice, favor, and honor must be placed in the balance, and God allowed to prevail. It is not the acquiring, but the confessing that should concern us. We should willingly endure being reviled before all the world as corrupt, a heretic, an apostate, or blasphemer and be persecuted, banished, burned at the stake, or otherwise killed, for then God's mercy is on us. Even if they were to take our life, they cannot take our faith and the truth from us. However, there are few in this respect who rage and behave bizarrely, like those do who compete to obtain the best and justice in worldly matters. There are also few who confess it correctly and on principle. We should lament and feel sorry for such a one, who through the undermining of the Gospel receives barriers to one's own salvation. Indeed, one should rather much more here, in God's eyes, worry and make an effort to avoid such damage to the soul, as the Moabites did for the sake of their own worldly goods and advantage, as said above. For it is lamentable when God's Word does not win and prevail; not just for the sake of the confessor, but for the sake of those who would have been saved by it. Thus, we see in the prophets, in Christ, and in the apostles such great sorrow and pity regarding the suppression of God's Word, though they were happy to undergo any manner of injustice and injury. For here there is another reason for winning this good, above all other goods. Yet no one should use force or keep the right of the Gospel by means of rage and irrationality, but rather should humble oneself before God as one who is not worthy that such a great thing could be done through one, and entrust everything to God's mercy with prayer and supplication. Thus, the first work of God is this: he has mercy on all who are willing to relinquish their own opinion, rights, wisdom, and all spiritual goods, and are willing to remain poor in spirit. These are the truly God-fearing people who do not think they are worthy of anything, small as it may be, but are willing to be naked and bare before God and the world. And whatever they have, they attribute to his grace alone, without any deserving on their part, and use them with praise, thanks, and fear, as if they belonged to someone else. They do not seek their own will, desire, praise, and honor but only his to whom they belong. Mary shows how much more joy God has in showing mercy, his noblest work, than that of its counterpart, his strength. Thus she says that this work endures unceasingly from generation to generation in those who fear God, but his strength endures to the third and fourth generation, which in the following verse has no time period or limit set on it, as we will see next.

The Second Work of God: Destroying Spiritual Pride

VI. He has shown strength with his arm, he has scattered the proud in the thoughts of their hearts (v. 51).

No one should be confused by my previous translation above of the phrase: "He has shown strength," while here I translate it as: "He shows strength." I have done this so that we will better understand the words that are not bound to any time, but rather clearly show God's works and ways, which he has always done, always does, and always will do. It would be similar if I were to say in German: "God is the kind of Lord whose works are such that he powerfully scatters the proud and is merciful to those who fear him."

God's "arm" in Scripture means his own power by which he works and acts without any creature acting as intermediary. This work is done quietly and in secret so that no one is aware of it until all is accomplished, so that this power or arm can only be understood or known through faith. Therefore, Isaiah complains (Isaiah 53:1) that too few have faith in this arm, saying: "Who has believed what we have heard? And to whom has the arm of the Lord been revealed?" This is the result of what is next described (Isaiah 53:2–3) as God working in secret and without any hint of power. Habakkuk also says (Habakkuk 3:4) that there were rays emitting from God's hands to show his mighty power, yet his "power lay hidden." How is this so?

When God works by means of one of his creatures, it is easy to identify where there is strength and where there is weakness. That is why we have the saying: "God helps those who help themselves." Whenever a prince wins a battle, it is said that God has defeated the enemy through him. If a person is eaten by a wolf or otherwise harmed, it is seen as caused by the creature. Thus God makes or breaks one creature by means of another. Whoever falls, falls, and whoever stands, stands. But it is different when God himself works with his own arm. Then a thing is destroyed before one knows it and, conversely, raised up before one knows it or sees it. Such works he does between both parts of the world, the godly and the wicked. He lets the godly become powerless and brought low so that everyone thinks that it is over for them, but in reality God is with them in all his power, yet so hidden and in secret that those who suffer the oppression do not feel it, but believe. There God's strength is complete and his arm is outstretched. For when the power of man is done, God's strength arrives, where faith is present and waits on him. And when the oppression is over, it becomes obvious how much strength there was in the midst of the hardship. Thus, Christ was powerless on the cross, yet despite this he accomplished the greatest act of power by overcoming sin, death, the world, hell, the devil, and all evil. In the same way, all martyrs have been strong and have overcome, as do all who today suffer and are oppressed. Therefore Joel says (Joel 3:10): "Let the weakling say, 'I am strong,'" but in faith and without sensing it until all is accomplished.

By contrast, God allows the other half of humankind to elevate themselves. He withdraws his power from them and allows them to puff themselves up on their own. For wherever man's power intrudes, God's power departs. And when they have puffed themselves up completely so that everyone thinks that they have won and prevailed, and when they themselves feel secure in their achievement, that is when God bursts their bubble and releases all the air. The fools do not realize that when they are puffing themselves up and growing strong that God has abandoned them and his arm is not with them. Their prosperity has had its day and bursts like a bubble as if it had never existed. The psalmist talks about this in Psalm 73:16–20, where he is amazed at how the evil can become so rich, secure, and powerful in the world. Finally he says: "But when I thought how to understand this, it seemed to me a wearisome task, until I went into the sanctuary of God; then I perceived their end. Truly you set them in slippery places; you make them fall to ruin. How they are destroyed in a moment, swept away utterly by terrors! They are like a dream when one awakes; on awaking you despise their phantoms." And in Psalm 37:35–36, it says: "I have seen the wicked oppressing, and towering like a cedar of Lebanon. Again I passed by, and they were no more; though I sought them, they could not be found."

It is because of our lack of faith that we are unable to wait a little longer until we, too, are able to see how the mercy of God is powerfully with those who fear him and the arm of God is firmly and powerfully against the proud. We faithless try to find God's mercy with our own hands and try in vain to touch the arm of God, and when we cannot, we think our cause is lost and our enemies have won, as if God's grace and mercy had abandoned us and his arm was against us. We do this because we do not know the works of God and therefore do not know him, his mercy, or his arm, because he must and will be known through faith. Sense and reason must be shut; the eye that troubles us should be plucked out and thrown away. These, therefore, are the two contrary works of God by which we learn that God is inclined to be far from the clever and wise and near to the foolish and to those who must bear up under injustice. But this makes God loving and worthy of praise; he brings comfort for our soul and body and all our powers.

Now let us consider the words: "He scatters the proud in the thoughts of their hearts." This destruction takes place, as we have said, even when they are at their most clever and secure in their own wisdom, for then God's wisdom is certainly never there. How could he better scatter them than to deprive them of his eternal wisdom and leave them to be filled with their own temporal, fleeting, and corruptible wisdom? Mary refers to "the proud in the thoughts of their hearts," namely, those who are pleased with their own opinions, thoughts, and reason, inspired by their own hearts and not by God, believing themselves to be the most accurate, best, and wisest. As a result, they elevate themselves above those who fear God by diminishing their opinions and abilities, putting them down and hounding them to the limit, claiming that their (i.e., the proud) opinion is the correct one and should prevail. And when they succeed, they brag and strut, as the Jews did with Christ, not seeing that their actions actually hurt and embarrass their cause, while Christ was exalted to glory. Therefore we see that this verse is talking about spiritual goods and how we can know God's work in both of its aspects. It shows us that we should gladly be poor in spirit and suffer injustice and allow our adversaries to prevail. They will not last long because the promise is too strong for them and they cannot escape the arm of God. They must be brought as low as they once were high, if only we would believe. But where there is no faith, God does not perform such works, and lets things go their own way, working through his creatures, as we have said above. Yet these are not his proper works by which he is made known, for the power of his creatures is intermingled in them. They are not the pure works of God, which are manifest when no one else works with him, but he alone. This happens when we are powerless and oppressed because of our status or opinion and allow God's power to work in us; those are the sublime works.

How masterfully Mary engages these false types. She does not look at their hands or their eyes, but into their hearts when she says "the thoughts of their hearts." Here she refers in particular to the enemies of divine truth, as the Jews were in their opposition to Christ and as Christians are today. These scholars and saints do not take pride in their clothing or demeanor; they pray, fast, preach, and study a lot, conduct Mass, behave humbly, and shun expensive clothes. They think that there is no better enemy of pride, wrong, or hypocrisy than they are; likewise, there is no greater friend of the truth and God. How can such holy, pious, and learned people possibly do any harm to the truth? Their polished outward appearance and show convince the masses. They have good hearts and mean well; they pray to God and have pity for Jesus, who was wrong and proud, and not as pious as they are. Matthew says of these people that "wisdom is vindicated by her children," meaning: "They are more righteous and wise than I am, divine wisdom itself; whatever I do is not right and I am mastered by them."

These are the most toxic, pernicious people on earth; their hearts an abyss of satanic pride for which there is no cure. They do not listen to what anyone has to say; it is of no concern to them. They leave all teaching to the poor sinners for whom such teaching is necessary, but not for them. John calls them "a brood of vipers" in Luke 3:7, as does Christ (Matthew 12:34). These are the truly guilty ones who do not fear God and deserve to have God scatter them for their pride because no one persecutes justice and wisdom more than they do, though ostensibly for the sake of God and righteousness. Therefore, they must be counted as the three foremost enemies of God on this side. For the rich are the least of these enemies; more dangerous are the powerful, but such "scholars" are the greatest because they provoke others. The rich destroy the truth from within, the powerful drive it away from others, but these learned people completely extinguish it and replace it with something else, the thoughts of their hearts, so that the truth can no longer rise. To the extent that the truth is itself better than the people among whom it dwells, so much worse are these scholars than the powerful and rich. Oh, God is their particular enemy, as they deserve!

The Third Work: Bringing Down the Powerful

VII. He has brought down the powerful from their thrones (v. 52).

This work and those that follow are easy to understand from the viewpoint of the two previous ones. For just as he scatters the wise and clever in their willfulness and discretion, upon which they rely, inflicting their pride on the God-fearing, who must be in the wrong and whose opinion and right must be condemned, which happens mainly for the sake of God's Word, so also he scatters the powerful and mighty with their power and authority, upon which they rely, inflicting their pride on the lowly and humbly pious, who must suffer harm, pain, death, and all kinds of evil at their hands. Just as he comforts those who suffer injustice and harm because of their status, truth, and witness, so also he comforts those who must suffer injury and evil. And to the extent he comforts the latter, to the same extent he terrifies the former. But all this will be known in faith and waited for to the end of days. He does not destroy them immediately, as they deserve, but allows them to continue on for a time until their power is at its height. If God does not support them, they cannot support themselves. They decline without fanfare, and the oppressed are raised up, also without fanfare, for God's strength is in them and it alone remains when the mighty have fallen.

Note, however, that Mary does not say that he breaks the thrones, but that "he has brought down the powerful from their thrones." She also does not say that he leaves the lowly in their lowly condition, but rather he lifts them up. For as long as the world stands, there must be authority, rule, power, and seats of power. But those who have them abuse them and use them against God to inflict injustice and violence on the godly (delighting in them and using them to elevate themselves), something that God will not tolerate for long because they do not use them in the fear of God to his honor and for the protection of justice. We see in all the history books and from experience how he raises up one kingdom and puts down another, lifts up one principality and destroys another, increases one population and decreases another, just as he did with Assyria, Babylon, Persia, Greece, and Rome, though they thought that they would rule forever. Nor does he destroy reason, wisdom, and justice, because they must remain if the world is to go on. However, he does destroy pride and the proud, who serve only themselves and are satisfied not to fear God, but persecute the godly and the divine justice by means of them and thus abuse God's good gifts, turning them against him.

Now in divine matters, the clever ones and proud scholars align themselves with the powerful to work against the truth, as it says in Psalm 2:2: "The kings of the earth set themselves, and the rulers take counsel together, against the Lord and his anointed. . . ." For the wise, powerful, and rich, namely, the world at its greatest and highest ability, will always go against the truth and justice. Thus, the Holy Spirit comforts with truth and justice through the words of this mother, so that they will not be deceived or afraid. Let these people be wise, mighty, and rich, it will not be for long. For if the saints and scholars together with the powerful, rulers, and the wealthy were not against, but were rather in favor of justice and truth, then what about wrongdoing? Who would suffer evil? No, the scholars, saints, powerful, great, and the wealthy and best in the world must strive together against God and what is right, and be on the devil's side, as it is written in Habakkuk 1:16: "for by them his portion is lavish, and his food is rich," meaning that the evil one has a taste for delicacies and eats only the best, most dainty, and choicest dishes, like a bear with honey. Thus the scholars and holy hypocrites, great lords, and the rich are the devil's choicest tidbits. On the other hand, Paul says in 1 Corinthians 1:28 that God chooses what the world discards: the poor, the lowly, naïve, humble, and despised. And in 1 Corinthians 3:7 he says that God allows the best part of the world to oppress the lowliest, so that we should know that our salvation does not lie with people, but solely with God's power and works. Therefore there is a lot of truth to the sayings: "The more people know, the worse they grow"; and "A prince is a rare thing in heaven"; and "Rich on earth, poor in heaven." For the learned and scholars will not give up the pride of their hearts, nor will the powerful stop oppressing others, and the rich will not stop being avaricious. And so it goes, on and on.

The Fourth Work: Exalting the Lowly

VIII. "and lifted up the lowly" (v. 52).

"The lowly" here does not mean the humble, but those that the world thinks are unsavory and worthless. It is the same word that Mary uses above to refer to herself when she says: "He has looked with favor on the lowliness of his servant." Indeed, those who are lowly of heart and nothing, and who do not seek greatness, are the truly humble.

The "lifted up" is not to be understood as awarding the lowly the status of those whom he has brought down. Likewise, when he shows mercy to those who fear him, he does not put them in the place of the learned or scholars (i.e., the proud), but gives them much, much more, for in God he gives them spiritual authority over all seats of power and might, as well as the ability to judge all knowledge here on earth and in heaven, since they will know more than the learned and the powerful. How this happens has already been discussed in the first section, so it is not necessary to repeat it. All of this is for the comfort of the suffering and to instill fear in tyrants, if only we had faith enough to believe it is so.

The Fifth and Sixth Works

IX. "he has filled the hungry with good things, and sent the rich away empty" (v. 53).

As we said above, "the lowly" are not those who are in a disgusting and worthless state, but those who are willing to suffer or be in such a state, especially if forced to be so as a result of God's Word or justice. Likewise, the hungry are not those who have little or no food to eat, but those who willingly suffer want, especially if forced to do so by God or the truth. What is lower, more worthless, and needier than the devil and the damned, who are tortured, starved, or slain as a result of their own evil deeds, as well as all who are lowly and in need against their will? Yet nothing helps, but only adds to their misery and makes it more unbearable. These are not the people that the Mother of God is talking about, but those who are one with God and God with them, who believe in him and put their trust in him.

On the other hand, how did wealth harm the holy fathers, Abraham, Isaac, and Jacob? What kind of barrier was David's throne for him, or Daniel's authority in Babylon? And what kind of barrier is wealth today to those with great status or wealth as long as they do not lose their hearts to it or seek self-sufficiency in it? "But," says Solomon in Proverbs 16:2, "the Lord weighs the spirit," meaning that he does not judge based on external appearance or form, whether rich, poor, high, or low, but according to the spirit and how it behaves within the person. Different types of people and distinctions between them will still remain, as will stations in this life on earth, but the heart should neither cling to them nor run from them; it should not cling to the high and mighty, nor shun the poor and lowly. As it says in Psalm 7:9 and 11: "you test the minds and hearts, O righteous God," and: "God is a righteous judge." People, however, judge according to outward appearances and that is why they are often wrong.

As above, these works are done in secret, so that no one knows about them until the end. A rich man is not aware of how utterly empty and miserable he is until he is dying or otherwise ruined. Then he sees how everything he has amounts to nothing, as it says in Psalm 76:5: "The stouthearted were stripped of their spoil; they sank into sleep. . . ." On the other hand, the hungry do not know how much they have until the end and they find truth in the words of Christ in Luke 6:21: "Blessed are you who are hungry now, for you will be filled." And, in the comforting words of promise of the Mother of God: "He has filled the hungry with good things." It is impossible for God to allow anyone who trusts him to die of hunger; all the angels would sooner come to feed that person. Elijah was fed by ravens (1 Kings17:6) and both he and Zarephath the widow subsisted on a handful of meal for many days (17:15). God will not forsake those who trust in him, which is why David says in Psalm 37:25: "I have been young, and now am old, yet I have not seen the righteous forsaken or their children begging for bread." Whoever trusts in God is righteous. Psalm 34:10 says: "The young lions suffer want and hunger, but those who seek the Lord lack no good thing." And Samuel's mother says in 1 Samuel 2:5: "Those who were full have hired themselves out for bread, but those who were hungry are fat with spoil."

Our unfortunate lack of faith continually prevents God from doing such works in us, as well as prevents us from either experiencing or knowing them. We would rather be full and have enough of everything before hunger and need arrive. We take care to stockpile against future hunger and need so that we will never need God or his works. What kind of faith is that, that trusts in God as long as you know and perceive you have provisions stored up to help yourself? Unbelief causes us to see God's Word, the truth, and justice as defeated while injustice triumphs; it causes us to remain silent, not to argue, speak out against or resist, letting things go as they will. Why? We worry that we too will be threatened and made poor, and that we will die of hunger and be eternally destitute. However, this is to value perishable goods above God and to make an idol of them, thus making us unworthy to hear or to understand the comfort of God's promise that he lifts up the lowly, brings down the mighty, fills up the poor, and empties the rich. And so we will never arrive at a knowledge of his works, without which there is no salvation and must be eternally damned, as it says in Psalm 28:5: "Because they do not regard the works of the Lord, or the work of his hands, he will break them down and build them up no more."

This is right because they do not believe his promises and consider him to be a frivolous, unreliable God. They do not trust in his Word enough to dare or begin anything; that is how little they regard his truth. Indeed, we should try and make an attempt based on his words. For Mary does not say he filled the full and lifted up the mighty, but "he has filled the hungry . . . and lifted up the lowly." In hunger you must have been brought to the edge of desperation to understand what hunger and need really are: that no provisions or help will come to you from others, but only from God; that this work is not possible for anyone else, but only for God. You should not only think and talk about being degraded, but arrive in such a state of humiliation and be stuck in it without help from anyone so that God alone can work, or at least welcome it and not shy away from it so that it can actually happen. That is why we are Christians and have the Gospel, which neither the devil nor people can tolerate, so that through it we experience need and humiliation so that God can also do his work in us. Consider yourself: if God were to fill you before you were hungry, or lift you up before you had been brought down, then he would be no different than an imposter who cannot deliver on promises made and everything the imposter does is a joke. However, Psalm 111:7 says: "The works of his hands are faithful and just." Even if he were to lift your need and degradation, or help in a minor case of need or humiliation, such works would be too meager for his divine power and majesty, as it says in Psalm 111:2: "Great are the works of the Lord, studied by all who delight in them." Now let us consider the opposite. If he were to shatter the rich before they became rich and mighty, how would he do it? First, they must become so rich and powerful that they, and everyone else, thinks that they are so secure that nobody can break them or oppose them, so sure are they of their position; as Isaiah says of them and of Babylon in Isaiah 47:8–9: "Now therefore hear this, you lover of pleasures, who sit securely, who say in your heart, 'I am, and there is no one besides me; I shall not sit as a widow or know the loss of children,' [i.e., the loss of power and help] both these things shall come upon you in a moment, in one day." Only then can God work in them. Thus he allowed Pharaoh to rise above the children of Israel and oppress them, as he says of himself in Exodus 9:16: "But this is why I have let you live: to show you my power, and to make my name resound through all the earth." The Bible is full of these examples that teach of nothing other than the Word and works of God, but reject the word and works of people.

See what a great comfort it is that not people, but God himself not only feeds the hungry, but fills and satisfies them. Mary says he fills them "with good things," namely, a fullness that is not harmful, but one that is helpful and beneficial and is good for both body and soul with all its powers. However, it also shows that the hungry were already bereft of good things and extremely needy. For, as stated above, riches here include all kinds of temporal goods that meet physical needs, but also make the soul glad. Likewise, hunger does not only mean food, but a lack of all temporal goods. A person can do without everything except food, so that almost all goods exist for the sake of supplying food, for no one can live without food even if they can live without clothing, house, gold, property, and other people. That is why Scripture highlights temporal goods that are most necessary in terms of need and utility and that are the most essential for sustenance. They also highlight the stingy and those who are envious of temporal goods, whom it calls "servants of their own appetites" (Romans 16:18), and about whom Paul says: "their god is the belly" (Philippians 3:19). How can one be any more strongly and trustingly incited to willingly endure hunger and poverty than through the splendid words of the Mother of God that God will fill the hungry with all good things? Whoever is not moved by these words and their honor and praise of poverty is certainly without faith and trust, like an unbeliever.

On the other hand, how could there be a greater condemnation of wealth and horrific shock to the rich than to say that God sends them away empty? Oh, how powerful and overwhelming are God's emptying and filling! How impotent is any earthly creature to assist or to advise! A person is terrified to hear that one's father has disowned one or that one has disappointed one's boss, but we powerful and rich do not feel terror when we hear that God has disowned us—and not just disowned us, but threatens to break us, humble us, and turn us away empty-handed! On the other hand, there is joy when one's father is benevolent and one's boss or lord is gracious, to the point where one relies on it so much that one even gives away one's own property and life. That is God's promise and such a powerful comfort, yet we neither use nor enjoy them, thank him, or rejoice in them. Oh, pitiful unbelief, hard as rock and firm as stone that it cannot feel such great things! Let this conclude what is to be said about the six works of God.

X. He has helped his servant Israel in remembrance of his mercy (v. 54).

After listing the works of God done in her and in all people, Mary returns to the beginning and to the main priority, concluding the Magnificat with the greatest work of God, the Incarnation of the Son of God. She openly admits that she is just a girl and the servant of the whole world, and professes that the work done in her was not just for her but for the good of all of Israel. Still, she divides Israel into two parts and only highlights the part that serves God. However, no one serves God who does not first allow him to be God and to work in him, as discussed above. Nevertheless, the phrase "service of God" (i.e., worship) has taken on such a negative meaning and usage that whoever hears it does not think of such works, but rather of the ringing of bells, the stone and wood in churches, incense, lighted candles, the mumbling in churches, gold, silk, and precious gems in the vestments of choirboys and celebrants, the chalices and monstrances, organs and paintings, processions and church attendance, and the worst, the mumbling lips and counting of rosary beads. Unfortunately, this is what service of God means now. God himself knows nothing of this, but it is all we know. We sing the Magnificat daily with loud voices and wonderful pomp, yet the more we sing it, the more we silence its true music and meaning. But the text is clear: if we do not experience and teach the works of God, there will be no service of God, no Israel, no grace, no mercy, no God, even if we were to sing ourselves to death, ring all the bells, and drag all of the world's good inside. God has commanded none of these things and therefore, undoubtedly, takes no pleasure in them.

Now, the Israel that serves God benefits from the Incarnation of Christ—his own beloved people for the sake of whom he became a human being, to save them from the power of the devil, sin, death, and hell and brings them to righteousness, eternal life, and salvation. That is the help of which Mary sings, as Paul says in Titus 2:14: "He it is who gave himself for us that he might redeem us from all iniquity and purify for himself a people of his own who are zealous for good deeds." And St. Peter says in 1 Peter 2:9: "But you are a chosen race, a royal priesthood, a holy nation. . . ." These are the riches of boundless, divine mercy that we have received by pure grace and not by merit. That is why Mary says "in remembrance of his mercy," and not "in remembrance of our merit and worthiness." We were certainly in need, but entirely unworthy. God's praise and honor is based on that and we must silence our boasting and impudence. Nothing he saw moved him, except that he was merciful and he wanted to make known his merciful name. But why does it say that he "remembered" instead of "regarded" his mercy? Because he had promised mercy, as the following verse shows. Now, he waited a long time to show it so that it seemed that he had forgotten about it, just as all his works seem like he is forgetting us, but when he came it was clear that he had not forgotten, but had intended all the while to fulfill his promise.

It is true that under the word "Israel" we understand the Jews and not the Gentiles, but because they would not accept him, he chose several out of their number, preserving the name Israel but making it a spiritual Israel from that point on. This was shown in Genesis 32:24–28, when the holy patriarch Jacob wrestled with the angel, who put his hip out of joint to show that his children should not boast of their fleshly birth, as do the Jews. He consequently received the name Israel, a name that he was to bear from then on, as patriarch Jacob of a fleshly line of children, but also as Israel, patriarch of a spiritual line, which is fitting because the word Israel means "a prince with God." That is a very high, holy name and contains in it the great miracle that, by the grace of God, a man prevailed so that God did what he wanted. In the same way, we see that through Christ, Christendom is united with God like a bride is with her bridegroom, so that the bride has rights and power over her bridegroom's body and all that he has. And all this happens through faith, so that people do what God wills, and God does what people will. Thus, "Israel" means a God-conformed and divinely powerful human being, one who is a lord in God, with God, and through God, able to do all things.

That is what Israel means. The Hebrew word *saar* means a lord or prince, and *El* means God. When you put them together, they become Israel (*El-saar*) in Hebrew. God wills such an Israel. Therefore, when Jacob had wrestled with the angel and won, the angel said to him (Genesis 32:28): "'You shall no longer be called Jacob, but Israel, for you have striven with God and with humans, and have prevailed.'" There is much more to be said on this subject, for Israel is an unusually profound mystery.

XI. According to the promise he made to our ancestors, to Abraham and to his descendants forever (v. 55).

In this verse all merit and overconfidence are brought down, and God's sheer grace and mercy are exalted, for God has not helped Israel on the basis of merit, but on the basis of his promise. He made the promise out of pure grace, and he fulfilled it out of pure grace. Therefore, St. Paul says in Galatians 3:17 that God gave the promise to Abraham four hundred years before he gave the law to Moses, so that no one could boast or say that one had earned or merited such grace and promise through the law or through the works of the law. The Mother of God praises and exalts this promise above everything else, attributing the incarnation of God solely to the divine, gracious, undeserved promise God made to Abraham.

The promise of God to Abraham is recorded primarily in Genesis 12:3 and 22:18 and is referred to in many other places as well. It says: "and in you all the families of the earth shall be blessed." These words of God are highly esteemed by St. Paul (Galatians 3:16) and all the prophets, as is appropriate. For through these words Abraham and all of his descendants were preserved and saved, and we too must all be saved through them. For here Christ is known and promised as the Savior of the world. This is the bosom of Abraham (Luke 16:22), in which all who were saved before Christ's birth were kept. Without these words of promise no one was saved, even though he had done all manner of good works. We will see this in the following.

First, it follows from these words of God that without Christ all the world is filled with sin and damnation and is cursed by its own deeds and knowledge. For when he says not some, but all generations should be blessed from Abraham's seed, then without Abraham's seed no nation will be blessed. Why would God promise salvation with such great earnestness and a precious oath if they were already saved and not clearly cursed? The prophets have derived and deduced many things: that all people are evil, complete liars, false, blind, and, in short, without God, so that in Scripture it is no great honor to be called a human being, since for God the name "human" is no different than the name "liar" or "faithless" in the eyes of the world. Humankind is so completely corrupt through the fall of Adam that the curse is inbred and an integral part of human nature and being.

Second, the seed of Abraham could not be born naturally of a man and a woman, for this birth is cursed and results in fruit that is cursed, as has been said. However, if this seed of Abraham were to deliver the entire world, which would in turn be blessed by it, as the words and oath of God declare, then the seed had to first be blessed, not touched or tainted by such a curse, but pure blessing, full of grace and truth (John 1:14). On the other hand, if God, who cannot lie, promised and swore that it should be Abraham's natural seed, that is, a natural, genuine child that would be born of flesh and blood, then this seed had to be a natural and genuine human being, of Abraham's flesh and blood. Here there is a contradiction: to be naturally of Abraham's flesh and blood, but not naturally born of a man and a woman. That is why he uses the term "your seed" (Genesis 22:18) and not "your child," so that it would be very clear and certain that it should be his natural flesh and blood, as is the seed. Everyone knows that a child does not need to be one's own natural child. Who can find a middle ground allowing God's Word and oath to stand, when there are such contradictory things opposing each other?

God himself has done this. He can fulfill what he promises, even if no one understands it before it happens. That is why his Word and work do not demand reason as its basis, but a pure and free faith. See how he combined the two. He raised up seed from Abraham, the natural son born to one of his daughters, a pure virgin, Mary, through the Holy Spirit, and without her lying with a man. There was no natural conception with its curse, nor could the curse touch this seed; and yet it is the natural seed of Abraham, as truly as any other of Abraham's children. Accordingly, it is the blessed seed of Abraham that sets the entire world free from its curse. For whoever believes in this seed, calls on it, confesses and clings to it, in him the curse is forgiven and all blessedness is his, as the words and oath of God says:

Luther's *Commentary on the Magnificat*

"In your seed shall all the nations of the world be blessed." In other words: "Everything that will be blessed must and should be blessed through this seed, otherwise it will not be blessed at all." Thus, it is the seed of Abraham that was not born from any of his sons, as the Jews expected and thought it would, but from one of his own daughters, Mary, alone.

This is what the sweet Mother of this seed means when she says that "he has helped his servant Israel . . . according to the promise he made . . . to Abraham and his descendants forever." She knew that the promise was fulfilled in her, which is why she said: "according to the promise he made" (v. 55) he has "helped his servant Israel, in remembrance of his mercy" (v. 54); merely remembering his merciful word of promise is enough. Here we find the foundation of the Gospel, and why all teaching and preaching drive people to faith in Christ and to the bosom of Abraham. For there is no other means or help available to grasp this blessed seed if faith is not present. Indeed, the entire Bible depends on this promise of God because everything in the Bible has to do with Christ. Furthermore, we see that all of the Old Testament fathers and the holy prophets have had the same faith and the same Gospel that we have, as Paul says in 1 Corinthians 10:1–4. They all were steadfast with a strong faith in this promise of God and in Abraham's bosom and were preserved by it, except that they believed in the future promised seed, and we believe in the seed that has already appeared and been given. However, all of it is the one true promise, and thus one faith, one spirit, one Christ, one Lord(Ephesians 4:4–5), today and for all time to eternity, as Paul says in Hebrews 13:8.

The fact that later on the Jews were given the law is not in accord with this promise, because it was given so that they could see their cursed nature better through the light of the law, and all the more fervently and ardently desire the promised seed of salvation, giving them an advantage over the heathen of the world. But they turned this advantage into a disadvantage and tried to fulfill the law on their own, and thus did not recognize their needy and cursed condition. Thus they shut the door on themselves, forcing the seed to pass on by. And they remain so to this day, though God willing not for long! Amen. This was the cause of the quarrel all the prophets had with them. For the prophets understood correctly the intention of the law: that one should by it recognize one's accursed nature and learn to call on Christ. Therefore they condemned all good works and the lives of the Jews that did not take this path. And so the Jews became angry with them and killed them, like those do who reject service to God, good works, and a good life, and like the hypocrites and graceless saints still do. There is a lot to be said about this.

But when Mary says: "to Abraham and to his descendants forever," we should understand "forever" to mean that such grace is to continue on through Abraham's seed, namely, the Jews, from that time on and through all time, until the Last Day. For though the vast majority were hardened, there are always some, few though they may be, who turn to Christ and believe in him. For this promise of God does not lie, that Abraham and his seed were the source of the promise, not for one year, and not for a thousand years, but for eternity, namely, from one generation to the next without stopping. That is why we should not be unkind to the Jews, because there may be future Christians among them and there are every day. They alone, not we Gentiles, have the promise that for all eternity there will be Christians among Abraham's seed who recognize the blessed seed. But our condition rests entirely on grace, without such a promise from God. And who knows where and when? If we lived Christian lives and led people to Christ with kindness, that would be good. But who wants to become a Christian when he sees them dealing with people in such an unchristian way? Not so, dear Christians. Tell them the truth in gentleness, and if they will not receive it, let them go their way. How many Christians are there that do not heed Christ or hear his Word, and are worse than the Jews and the heathen? Yet we let them go in peace, fall at their feet, and even pray to them like idols! Let us stop here for this time and pray to God for a correct understanding of the Magnificat, one that is not just lofty words, but that burns and lives in body and soul. May Christ grant us this through the intercession of his dear Mother Mary and for her sake! Amen.

EPILOGUE TO THE MAGNIFICAT

Finally, I return again to you, your Grace, and ask that Your Serene Highness might forgive my presumption. For although I know that in your youth Your Serene Highness received daily instruction and guidance, I still cannot relinquish my duty and loyalty as your subject or my very real concern and thoughts for the welfare of Your Serene Highness. For we all hope that at some future time, depending upon God's grace and beneficence, the rule of Saxony will fall into your hands. If it succeeds, that will be a huge and delicate project, but a dangerous one and full of misery if it does not. We shall hope for the best in all things and pray, but nevertheless fear for and take care against the worst.

Your Serene Highness should consider that in all of Scriptures God never allowed a heathen king or duke to be praised at any time to the ends of the earth, but always allowed them to be punished. That is a very great and fearsome portrayal of overlords. Even among the people of Israel, who were his own people, he never found a king who was praiseworthy or who was not deserving of punishment. Furthermore, among the tribe of Judah, which is the source of the entire human race and which God raised above all others and loved above all others, he only praised a few of their kings, not more than six. And the most noteworthy among them, King David—who had no equal before him, next to him, or after him among the kingdoms of the world, though he was full of the fear of God and exhibited wisdom in all his deeds, which he did only by God's command, not leading or commanding by his own reason—faltered numerous times. And although the Scriptures could not reproach his kingdom, the people nevertheless experienced hardship despite David. The Scriptures did not blame David, but rather the people, saying that God was angry with his people and allowed David, a holy man, to be moved by the devil, so that because of his deeds seven thousand people died of the plague (2 Samuel 24).

All of this God had ordained to frighten the authorities and keep them fearful, and to keep their misdeeds before them. For the greatest good, the greatest honor, the greatest power, the greatest favor, even the greatest flatterers without whom no lord can exist, are at the same time bound by the heart of a lord while attempting to challenge it—due to pride, the forgetting of God, the misdeeds of the people, and the general use of lust, wickedness, arrogance, and idleness, in short, all kinds of injustice and lack of virtue, so that clearly no castle or city could be besieged or attacked as harshly. Whoever does not heed such an example and make the fear of God into a stronghold and defense, how will he prevail? For if a lord or an authority does not love his people and keeps his concerns to himself, as if he himself does not have only good days, but needs improvement just as much as his people, then it is all over for him because his authority and rule only leads to the ruin of his own soul. And it will not help him to establish great worship services, cloisters, altars, or this or that, because God will demand an account of him for his position and his office and not allow him to turn to anything else for help.

Therefore, my gracious Lord and Duke, I recommend the Magnificat to Your Serene Highness, especially the fifth and sixth verses, which provide a summary in the middle. I also ask and mildly recommend to Your Serene Highness that for all of your days you will fear nothing more on the earth, even in hell, than what the Mother of God here calls the "disposition of one's heart." For that is the greatest, closest, mightiest, most pernicious enemy of all people and primarily of overlords; namely, reason, good intentions or discretion, from which all advice and regimes must draw. And Your Serene Highness cannot be safe from it if you do not always challenge prudence and follow in the fear of God. I do not just mean advice given to Your Serene Highness, but for all those who sit in counsel. Should no advice be heeded and should no one trust advice? What then?

May Your Serene Highness not ignore the prayers of the monks or of the priests, as is now the practice, and rely on and trust the prayers of other people, neglecting one's own prayers. Rather, Your Serene Highness should exhibit free and decisive courage and not be timid, and should talk to God by himself in his heart or in a secret place, and throw his keys down before him and urge him with his own counsel, such as: "See, my God and Father, it is because of your work and order that I have been born to and created for this position. That no one can deny. And you yourself know it too. If I am worthy or unworthy, I am, in any case, as you and everyone can see. Therefore, my Lord and Father, I ask that I be able to preside over these people to your honor and usefulness. Do not let me follow my own reason, but you be my reason."

And let whatever happens happen, according to God's command. Because of such a good prayer and disposition, God showed himself to Solomon, who also had prayed a prayer like the one I have translated here, so that Your Serene Highness may use it as an example and in the end keep it, awakening a comforting confidence in God's grace. Thus both remain, the fear of God and his mercy, as the fifth verse says. I hereby commend myself to Your Serene Highness, who should commend his blessed kingdom to God. Amen.

1 KINGS 3:5–14

How King Solomon prayed to God a noble prayer, providing a good example for all lords and rulers, from the Book of Kings.

Luther's *Commentary on the Magnificat*

In the city of Gibeon God appeared to Solomon in a dream during the night and said to him: "Ask me for something. What would you have me give you?" And Solomon said: "My God, you have bestowed great favor on David, my father, who walked with you in great truth and justice, and his heart was right with you, and you have retained for him this great favor that you have given him a son who now sits on his throne today."

"Now loving God, my Lord, you have made me, your servant, king in place of my father David, though I am but a child who does not know in from out. Thus, I am your servant in the midst of a great people that is so numerous that it cannot be reckoned in number."

"So, give me an attentive heart, O Lord—one that hears you and listens when you speak—so that I may govern your people and discern between good and evil; for who is able to judge such a large and bold people?"

God was pleased with these words and what Solomon had asked for, and said to him: "It is good that you have not asked for long life, riches, or the death of your enemies, but for the gift of discernment and understanding in order to hear how you should rule. See, I will give you what you ask: a wise and discerning heart the likes of which no one has seen before or will ever see again. Furthermore, the things that you did not ask for I will give you as well. You will have riches and glory beyond that of any king as long as you live. And if you walk in my ways and keep my commandments, as your father David did, I will also lengthen your days."

4

Bach on the Magnificat

BACH'S JOURNEY TO THE MAGNIFICAT IN E-FLAT MAJOR (BWV 243A)

IN MAY OF 1723, Bach began his twenty-seven-year tenure as cantor at the *Thomaskirche* (Church of St. Thomas) in Leipzig. For him, this was in some ways a demotion in career prestige. Bach had been the court musician in both Weimar and Anhalt-Köthen before coming to Leipzig. Both positions carried greater prestige than the position of church cantor. Moreover, Bach was actually the third choice for the post, after Georg Philipp Telemann and Johann Christoph Graupner. Because the first two turned down the post, the Leipzig city council voted for Bach. City councilman Abraham Christoph Platz concluded, "If we cannot get the best, then we will have to settle for average."[1] Little did they know that their "average" choice would turn out to be one of the most significant composers in all of music history.

The Leipzig post was enormous and demanding, involving teaching at the church school, playing the organ, training the choir, and composing music for the two principal Leipzig churches, the *Thomaskirche* and the *Nikolaikirche* (Church of St. Nicholas), as well as supervising and training the musicians at three others. Today, a post like this would probably be the work of three or four people!

---

1. Fischer, *Johann Sebastian Bach*, 82.

Bach on the Magnificat

A significant part of Bach's duties was to produce sacred cantatas to enhance worship throughout the changing seasons of the Christian church year. Bach not only dutifully wrote music for the worship services but also decided to write a yearly cycle of cantatas—one per Sunday. Bach completed two of these cycles—more than one hundred cantatas, a prolific amount of music—during his first two years in Leipzig. In his first year, he also produced the monumental *St. John Passion*, the first of the passions that he wrote, the most famous being the *St. Matthew Passion*, written in 1727. In all, he wrote literally hundreds of cantatas, of which about 60 percent have survived.

Most choral music in the centuries preceding Bach was written for a normal range of four voice parts—soprano, alto, tenor, bass. Writing for more than four voices was less common. Yet in the first weeks of Bach's new post, a funeral was held for the postmaster's widow and, probably eager to please his new employers and demonstrate his compositional prowess, Bach wrote his five-voice funeral motet, *Jesu, meine Freude* (Jesus, my joy) for that service.

In less than one month during the 1723 Christmas period, Bach had to write music for seven different feast days. Probably the most significant composition during that period was the *Magnificat* in E-flat Major. Written for the Vespers service on Christmas Day in the *Nikolaikirche*, Bach also wrote the *Magnificat* for five voice parts—soprano 1, soprano 2, alto, tenor, and bass—again possibly to gain favor with his new employers. At that point in Bach's career, the *Magnificat* was also one of his largest works. The *Magnificat* was sung in German on regular Sundays, but in Latin on feast days, and written in a concerted style with orchestra, chorus, and soloists.

Earlier Baroque examples of settings of the *Magnificat* text from Luke, notably those by Buxtehude and Schütz, had begun to treat the various verses of the text as separate movements, as opposed to the earlier and more through-composed examples by composers such as Palestrina, Gabrieli, and Monteverdi. Bach's work certainly treats each verse of the text as a different movement, and each has its own distinct material, except that the second half of the final chorus employs the same material as the opening movement, thus bringing it to a unified close.

Bach did not need to write a *Magnificat*, because other composers' versions were available to him in the music library, one by his predecessor in Leipzig, Johann Kuhnau. Following a local Christmas tradition dating back to the Late Middle Ages, Kuhnau's *Magnificat* includes four *Laudes*

(Lauds), essentially cradle songs or lullabies. Local custom dictated that the Lauds were to be sung by a separate "angelic" choir from the gallery of the church. The Lauds form a summary of Christmas in miniature.

Choosing to write his own *Magnificat* instead, Bach conceived his on a grand scale, requiring five soloists, a five-voice choir, and an unusually large orchestra for its time, consisting of three trumpets, two recorders (the default instrument for keys with flats), two oboes doubling on the *oboe d'amore* (oboe of love), strings, and continuo. In its splendor and jubilation, the piece anticipates the great choruses of his later works, such as the Mass in B Minor. The work is divided into twelve movements from the text of the Magnificat. Each verse is set as a separate musical movement, but none of them are built to any sort of standard pattern or form; there are no *da capo* arias with ABA form (the first section being repeated), no recitatives, and no "big" choruses of the sort that he would have used to open a cantata, for example. Each of the twelve movements is a tiny musical gem whose only purpose is to exhibit its text with the utmost conviction, clarity, and vividness. It alternates between exciting and vibrant choruses, mostly fugal and employing *tutti* (all play), and tender, reflective movements for soloists and much reduced orchestral forces.

Here is the full layout of all the movements:

Number	Latin Title	Key	Forces Required
I.	*Magnificat anima mea*	E♭ major	Chorus
II.	*Ex exsultavit spiritus meus*	E♭ major	Soprano 2 solo
III.	*Quia respexit humilitatem*	C minor	Soprano 1 solo
IV.	*Omnes generationes*	G minor	Chorus
V.	*Quia fecit mihi magna*	B♭ major	Bass solo
VI.	*Et misericordia*	F minor	Alto/tenor duet
VII.	*Fecit potenitam*	A♭/E♭ major	Chorus
VIII.	*Deposuit potentes*	G minor	Tenor solo
IX.	*Esurientes implevit bonus*	F major	Alto solo
X.	*Suscepit Israel*	C minor	Women's trio
XI.	*Sicut locutus est*	E♭ major	Chorus
XII.	*Gloria Patri*	E♭ major	Chorus

The basic structure of the *Magnificat* in E-flat Major is comprised of three groups of one chorus, two or three movements for solo voices in related keys, and a final group of the last two choruses. Here is a layout of the groups:

Group 1:

   I. Chorus

   II. Soprano 2 solo

   III. Soprano 1 solo

Group 2:

   IV. Chorus

   V. Bass solo

   VI. Duet for alto and tenor

Group 3:

   VII. Chorus

   VIII. Tenor solo

   IX. Alto solo

   X. Trio for women

Final group:

   XI. Chorus

   XII. Chorus

In the last movement of each group, Bach increasingly adds to the number of solo voices (see bold type above): Group 1 ends with a solo soprano voice (Movement III: *Quia respexit*), Group 2 ends with a duet sung by alto and tenor soloists (Movement VI: *Et misericordia*), and Group 3 ends with a trio for three female voices (Movement X: *Suscepit Israel*). Given Bach's attention to things Trinitarian, it is probably no accident that Bach pays homage in this way to the Father, Son, and Holy Spirit in the first three groups. The final group of two choruses serves to release the tension that Bach has built into the overall structure of the *Magnificat*. As noted, Bach often wrote "SDG" (*Soli Deo gloria*, To God alone be the glory) at the very end of a piece, and this attitude prevailed throughout his entire compositional life.

Honoring the local custom, Bach also included the four Lauds, hymns in both Latin and German. Musicologist Robert Marshall believes that the

Lauds of Bach—always both a preacher and teacher—seem to survey four historical styles of composition:[2]

1. The first Laud uses Martin Luther's Christmas hymn, *Vom Himmel hoch* (From Heaven above), and is an a cappella chorale, using the hymn tune as a *cantus firmus* (fixed melody) motet in strict *stile antico* (the "old style"). Palestrina and other composers of the Renaissance wrote in this style.

2. *Freut euch und jubiliert* (Rejoice and be glad) is polyphonic, with an independent basso continuo and pairs of voices moving in parallel motion. This style harkens back to early Baroque practice, in such works as Claudio Monteverdi's motets and an earlier setting of the same text (1603) by Seth Calvisus, himself a Thomaskantor in Leipzig in the early seventeenth century.

3. *Gloria in excelsis Deo* (Glory to God in the highest) is less polyphonic, has an obbligato violin part, and proceeds in a basically chordal fashion. It is reminiscent of Giacomo Carissimi's later Italian style, as cultivated by the Thomaskantors Johann Schelle, Kuhnau, and others.

4. *Virga Jesse* (Rod of Jesse) is the most contemporary in style, being written in florid operatic duet for soprano and bass soloists with continuo. It sounds almost like a lullaby at the cradle. Problematic in this movement is that the last page of the manuscript was missing. Contemporary editors had to finish by interpolating what they thought Bach might have done. In the Novello performing score of the *Magnificat* in E-flat Major, the Lauds are placed where each should be sung. However, the fact that they are grouped together at the back of the original manuscript, with notations in the score as to where they should be placed, seems to indicate that they were not originally planned as part of the work, but added as an afterthought. One possibility is that Bach may have been originally planning to use Kuhnau's *Magnificat*, but instead decided to write his own and bow to the Leipzig tradition of angelic choirs helping to tell the Christmas story.

---

2. Marshall, *Music of Johann Sebastian Bach*.

Bach on the Magnificat

THE MAGNIFICAT IN E-FLAT MAJOR: INDIVIDUAL MOVEMENTS

What follows is an interpretation of all movements of Bach's *Magnificat* in E-flat Major. A brief summary of Luther's comments about each verse of the text from the Gospel of Luke, with the verses given in both Latin and English, is provided for reference prior to the interpretation of the corresponding movement in Bach's composition. This format will be helpful in preparing to listen to each of the movements in Bach's *Magnificat*.

Movement I: Magnificat anima mea (Chorus)

Magnificat anima mea Dominum,
My soul magnifies the Lord, (Luke 1:46)

Luther's focus on this verse is on the Latin word *magnificat*. Mary's song glorifies God solely because of who God is. Glorifying God strengthens faith, comforts those in need, and frightens those who believe they are self-sufficient, those who think they have no need of God. Mary does not magnify herself, but gives all the glory to God alone for the miracle she is soon to experience.

Trumpets! Bach's *Magnificat* opens with a brilliant fanfare using three trumpets. Trumpet-like instruments have been used for centuries and centuries as "calls"—calls to worship, calls to battle, and introductions for presidents and royalty. Perhaps the first "trumpet" was the shofar of ancient origin, made of a horn, traditionally that of a ram, and used for Jewish religious purposes. Like the bugle and the early Baroque trumpets, the shofar lacked pitch-altering devices. All pitch control was done by varying the player's embouchure. During Bach's time, the trumpet was also valveless and very difficult to play. The early music movement, a twentieth-century revitalization of playing music in the style of its original composer and with instruments of the period, has revived the natural-tone trumpet in spite of modern conventions. The most famous and brilliant use by Bach is in the Brandenburg Concerto no. 2, in which the trumpet soars up to high F, two and a half octaves above middle C!

The *Magnificat's* opening instrumental fanfare gradually rises in pitch and brilliance. An English cognate of *magnificat*, "magnificent," describes the mood. Measures IX–XI have the trumpet rising scale-wise from a lower E♭ to high E♭, almost at the top of the baroque trumpet's range. The basic structure is ABA, the A sections using the exact same motive. The harmonic progression is typical, starting in the home key of E-flat major and moving to related keys, such as B♭ major and C minor. When the B section reaches the darker key of G minor, the melodic motion is an upward motive related to the trumpet's opening motive. The ascent may signify Mary's praise of God rising in intensity as she glorifies God for who he is and as she realizes the magnitude of the gift of being the Mother of Jesus. In addition, this also foretells some of what is coming in the *Magnificat*—that "the lowly shall be exalted." Luther had also addressed this concept of the lowly maiden being exalted but feeling unworthy of the position God has placed in front of her as well as within her.[3] The bubbling of excitement in Mary's soul matches beautifully the rising motives of the first movement. As a "horde of witnesses," the chorus also uses these motives to magnify Mary's joy.

Movement II: Et exultavit spiritus meus (Solo for Soprano 2)

et exsultavit spiritus meus in Deo salutari meo.
and my spirit has rejoiced in God my Savior. (Luke 1:47)

Luther notes how Mary's praise begins by focusing on God himself before listing any of God's works and blessings. Those who properly praise God do not do so out of self-interest but praise him solely because he is good. They see nothing more than his pure goodness and on that account alone are joyful and glad. Mary's joyful attitude is as if she says to God, "I do not seek what you have; I seek you."

The spirit of the two Latin words *exaltavit* and *exsultavit* are both used in the *Magnificat*. Movement VIII demonstrates *exaltavit*, a transitive verb that takes a direct object, as in exalting a king, thereby juxtaposing images of the proud being cast down while the lowly are exalted. Here in Movement II, *exsultavit* is an intransitive verb, meaning "to be in a state of jubilation." Mary has been exalted by God and exults in God's gift.

3. *LW* 21:297–358.

Bach on the Magnificat

Almost all Baroque music has some kind of dance underpinning. One of the most common is a dance in three-quarter time, such as the *courante*, a running dance; the *gigue* (jig); or the minuet, which bespeaks of courtly elegance. Movement II has the underpinning of this kind of elegant but sturdy dance. In rather Trinitarian fashion, Bach sets the first part of the text, *et exsulavit spiritus meus* (and my spirit has rejoiced), three times before setting the last half, *in Deo salutari meo* (in God my savior). The musical motive of the movement is jumps of a third upward, first heralded by the arpeggiated trumpet fanfare. In this movement, Mary demonstrates the exaltation by God, which causes her to exult. This movement emphasizes *in Deo* and *salutari*. The longest held notes, a full bar each, are on the syllable "-de" in *Deo* and "-ta" in *salutari*. Luther had said that this phrase reveals God as the giver of this great gift, causing Mary's spirit to be in "elegant exultation."

Laud 1: Chorus

Vom Himmel hoch da komm ich her.
From heaven above to earth I come.
Ich bring' euch gute neue Mär.
I bring you good new tidings.
Der guten Mär bring' ich so viel,
I bring so much good tidings
davon ich sing'n und sagen will.
of which I sing and will speak.

In the first Laud, the full melody of Luther's hymn is sung by the sopranos as a *cantus firmus* (fixed melody) in long notes, which has a sense of grandeur, almost stentorian. In other pieces by Bach, this type of line for an instrument would have been played by a trumpet or an oboe, both capable of soaring over the rest of the parts. Luther's opening melodic line is a descending scale, obviously stating the fact that the tidings come down from God in heaven above. The other parts are fugal and use much quicker notes (eighth and quarter notes). The motive for the other parts mirrors each of the lines of the hymn in the style of a chorale fugue, a form used extensively in the Baroque era, primarily in a composition for organ. In fact, this Laud could easily be played by a group of instruments instead of being sung by voices. The fugal voices give the impression of almost dancing around each new line of the hymn in a joyous, robust fashion.

Movement III: Quia respexit humilitatem (Solo for soprano 1)

> *Quia respexit humilitatem ancillae suae; ecce enim ex hoc . . . beatam me dicent.*
> For he has regarded the lowliness of his handmaiden: for behold, henceforth
> [all generations—Movement IV] will call me blessed. (Luke 1:48)

After Mary praises God with a simple, pure spirit, not presuming to deserve his gifts, she then praises his goodness and his works. As Mary considers her situation, she praises God for regarding her and choosing her in spite of her low estate.

This movement, in the related key of C minor, has Mary speaking words of her amazement with the wonders God has done by exalting a lowly, young girl such as herself. The key of C minor is often associated with a deep and serious pathos, a specific example of *Affektenlehre*.[4] The movement is in two parts. The melodic figure in the first part is a descending scale in a humble, bowing fashion. The bass line rises in a short scale, but then drops down a large interval. The most dramatic use of this figure occurs immediately in the first and second measures, with the bass dropping down the large dissonant interval of a seventh. Here Bach interprets the words beautifully. Mary bows and realizes the gift comes from above; she also has deep humility before God. The oboe plays alongside Mary's words in duet with the soprano. The text is introspective, but the oboe invites the listener into Mary's private moment. The inward mood even seems a little unnerving. Mary knows exactly where the gift comes from, but realizes the gravity of the fact that she will be blessed by all generations to come. The mood of the second part, "For behold all will call me blessed," indicates not only disbelief but also excitement. The word *ecce* (behold) is repeated four times in two groups, the motive rising upward with the second group even higher in pitch. Repeating *ecce* suggests Mary is thinking, "Really? Is this happening to me?!" Bach finishes the rest of the text, *ecce enim ex hoc beatam me dicent* [*omnes generationes*] (for behold, henceforth [all generations] will call me blessed), with a rich, descending line as Mary, although excited, still has a sense of humility. Movement III segues, without pause, to Movement

---

4. See page 19.

IV, *Omnes generationes* (all generations), completing the text of Mary's awe at what God has done now and for the future.

Movement IV: Omnes generationes (Chorus)

Omnes generations
All generations (Luke 1:48)

It is because of *what God has done for her* that all generations will call Mary blessed. Luther interprets "all generations" to mean that Mary will be honored for the blessings she received from God by each successive line of believers from one generation to the next.

Fast and furious! Bach powerfully portrays the words of Movement IV. The text, *omnes, omnes* (all, all), is repeated very quickly; this movement contrasts starkly with the previous one as Bach practically hurls the text at the listener. In each vocal part's entrance, *omnes* is repeated twice on a single pitch, which is followed by a fast and furious ascending melisma (a long melodic line with many moving sixteenth notes), signifying even more deeply that this is for *all* generations to come. In each of the repetitions of the text the chorus sings in *stretto* (Italian for "stressed"), and the piece sounds stressed! In every single bar on every eighth-note beat, *omnes* charges ahead. The melisma in fast sixteenth notes pushes even further the notion that the number of generations to come is vast. Probably the most dramatic moment occurs in measure 24, when the chorus abruptly halts. The typical ending of almost every piece from 1600–1900 is dominant-tonic (V–I). In the key of G minor, the pitches of the tonic are G-Bb-D, and the dominant pitches would be D-F#-A. Stopping a piece on the dominant leaves the listener hanging and begging for resolution. Bach halts here, not on the regular dominant chord, but rather a dominant ninth chord, a chord built from the bottom up, 1–3–5–7–9. In this harmonic moment, the pitches are D-F#-A-C-Eb. The dissonance created by a D together with an Eb is almost harsh. Leaving the listener in this way, Bach's chord is even more pregnant, much more so than a regular dominant chord. Truly, the dissonance is so powerful that it simply must be resolved! After this most dramatic moment, for the first time all voice parts sing *omnes* in unison rhythm, again portraying that all generations to come will call Mary "blessed."

Movement V: Quia fecit mihi magna (Solo for bass)

Quia fecit mihi magna qui potens est, et sanctum nomen eius.
For he that is mighty has done great things to me, and holy is his name. (Luke 1:49)

The "great things" of which Mary speaks in verse 49 are all based on her being chosen to become the Mother of God, through which so many great and good things were given to her. And it is through her becoming the Mother of God that she has a peerless place among all of humankind. Mary again attributes everything to God's grace, not to her own merit.

Gracious and flowing, rhythmic and grounded, *Quia fecit* exudes both strength and gentleness. An ostinato bass line (a bass line that is "obstinate" and is repeated many times) grounds the movement, and of course the fundamental for any harmonic movement is the bass motion. The English cognate, "obstinate," indicates that the piece has an almost inexorable quality; God's gift to Mary will endure. God is magnified, yet holy, which is characteristic of worship and veneration. God is all-powerful and Mary certainly understands that, as she will bear the Son of God as a virgin, which seems impossible. Mary accepts the challenge before her and, perhaps, is on her knees realizing, once again, the blessing and magnitude of God.

While the full motive is longer, Bach uses the first eight notes to define the piece. The opening instrumental bass line is repeated over and over, both in the instrumental bass line and in the voice, a total of sixteen times. In B-flat major, the harmonic motion is basically static and moves only briefly to G minor, the key that shares the same key signature of B-flat major. That in itself implies fundamental power. Bach does not need to move far away from the fundamental harmony. He uses word painting in this section of the text. For example, the opening statement of *potens* (mighty) is an elongated melisma that descends and ascends, painting a picture of the power of God actively moving between heaven and earth.

Laud 2: Chorus

Freut euch und jubiliert.
Rejoice and be glad.

> *Zu Bethlehem gefunden wird*
> In Bethlehem is found
> *das herzeliebe Jesulein.*
> the beloved little Jesus.
> *Das soll euer Freud und Wonne sein.*
> There shall be your hope and joy.

Joy and jubilation! In the second Laud, the ascending line of the soprano reaches high B-flat, the very top range of a soprano voice, almost immediately. The piece is polyphonic with independent voices. Yet the main motive, three ascending quarter notes, always occurs each with a second voice. This is a typical figure found especially in early Baroque music. Monteverdi used it in his motets and Sethus Calvisius (1603), himself a Thomaskantor like Bach, employed it in a setting of this very text. Knowledgeable in all styles of composition, Bach paints the mood much as Calvisius did. The word *euer* in German is the plural form of "you." Thus all people are included in this joyful movement. Almost every time the motive occurs, it is a jubilant ascending line. Bach's intention may be that all people shall be jubilant at the announcement of the birth of Jesus.

Movement VI: Et misericordia (Duet for solo alto and tenor)

> *Et misericordia eius a progenie in progenies timentibus eum.*
> And his mercy is on them that fear him throughout all generations. (Luke 1:50)

God's mercy is for those who fear God. The opposite of fearing God is to boast about what one has in life, be it human wisdom, might, or riches. The problem is not with wisdom, might, or riches per se, but with the attitude of one's heart toward them. Those who fear God know that whatever they have in life that is good must be attributed to God alone.

Bach describes the meaning and mood of this text beautifully. The key is F minor, which historically indicates both a foreboding and plaintive quality. The mood is plangent and immediately evokes sadness. In this duet, the voices never sing as a single voice, implying that, once again, God's mercy is for all who fear him. The use of the alto and tenor—the lowest female voice and the highest male voice—brings the singers and the sound incredibly close. Bach may have done this to indicate people huddling together in fear.

Immediately, the bass line seems ominous as it moves up and down by octaves, the main motive for the bass line for almost the entire piece. It almost feels like a dirge because of the repetition, but also again has an inexorable quality. The horizontal motion of the bass line is chromatically descending, which is often used to symbolize grief. The timbre is equally haunting with muted violins plus recorders. Muting a violin takes away some of its brilliance and creates a more intimate color. The only time the bass line changes is in measures 30–31, where the bass ominously repeats a single note three times. Given the up and down of the bass line thus far, the change is dramatic. The word at that moment is *timentibus* (fearful). Coupled with that, the tenor sings an incredibly tight, chromatically descending line to bring it back to F minor. The movement is both beautiful and yet unsettling to those who do not fear God.

Movement VII: Fecit potentiam (Chorus)

Fecit potentiam in brachio suo, dispersit superbos mente cordis sui.
He has shown strength with his arm, and has scattered the proud
in the imagination of their hearts. (Luke 1:51)

God shows strength with his "arm" by working directly on the lives of the proud. This he does in a hidden way, in secret. Suddenly, as if out of nowhere, the result of God's secret, hidden work becomes known: God strikes down the puffed-up, arrogant thoughts of the proud. As a result, the proud are deflated and brought low.

Strength is immediately apparent in this chorus, as four of the five parts move in block chords. It almost seems like pounding or a big gust of wind! There is no question that Bach is saying that God is in charge and willfully scatters the proud. While four voices (parts) sing in these block chords, one voice moves melismatically in sixteenth notes. Maybe that is the proud one being scattered. Usually in a power situation, one person controls the rest. Four against one is pretty powerful as the block chords continue throughout the piece, seeming to say, "You are not powerful over us!" God is indeed in charge. The text for the "proud" line is either *potentiam* (power) or *dispersit* (scatters). Thus, God is powerful and he does the scattering.

Because of the long running sixteenth notes, it is almost as if the proud one is running away.

One of the most fascinating uses of the word *dispersit* occurs just before the final adagio. The word is passed from soprano 1 to soprano 2 to alto to tenor, each voice starting the exchange before the previous voice is finished. When the bass finally has its turn, all voices in short, dramatic notes sing the word *superbos* (proud). God seems to be swatting away the proud! In the final measures, sung very slowly, Bach brings in three royal trumpets in a high *tessitura* (pitch level) as if to say one last time that God on high is the one who is most powerful.

Laud 3: Chorus

Gloria in excelsis Deo, et in terra pax hominibus bona voluntas.
Glory to God in the highest, and on earth peace and good will to all.

Compared to the previous Lauds, this one consists of block chords with all voices singing the same thing at the same time, resulting in a prevailing unity. Most striking in this movement is the repetition three times of *Gloria in excelsis Deo* (Glory to God in the highest). Once again Bach seems to be invoking God as Trinity—Father, Son, and Holy Spirit. This is more evident because the emphasis is on long quarter notes as *Deo* is sung each time. The mood is exuberant and joyful, almost bouncing. When the text changes to *et in terra pax* (and on earth peace), the metric motion slows down to mostly quarter notes, evoking the peaceful quality of the text.

Movement VIII: Deposuit potentes (Solo for tenor)

Deposuit potentes de sede, et exaltavit humiles.
He has cast down the mighty from their seats, and exalted the lowly.
(Luke 1:52)

Just as the proud were brought down in verse 51, here the same happens to the powerful—to mighty rulers who do not use their power wisely insofar as they do not fear or honor God when carrying out their duty of administering justice among the people. These rulers too are cast down from their seats of power. In contrast, God lifts up the lowly, not in the sense of giving them the status of worldly power, but rather in the sense that they are lifted up in faith, knowing that God is their God and that he comforts them no matter what their circumstances.

In *Deposuit* Bach aligns the music to clearly interpret Mary's words of casting down the mighty and exalting the lowly. Once again, Mary is aware of her position in life and realizes the power of God to deal with both the mighty and the lowly. Perhaps one of Bach's most dramatic movements, there is no doubt how he interprets the text. With an almost crashing gesture, the tenor sings the word *deposuit* (cast down) with fast, descending scales. As if to show the power of God, Bach ends this phrase with an abrupt upward jump. This interval is always dissonant, jumping an augmented fourth or a seventh, thus practically tossing away the mighty. The gesture is almost like a finger flicking a bug off one's shoulder. In contrast, on the word *exaltavit* the musical line rises gradually with quick melismas. The fast sixteenth notes seem to bubble with excitement, yet the rising line deliberately takes several measures, demonstrating a strength and determination in life; as Luther said, "make a fist of life." Indicating even more strength, Bach has all the upper strings dashing both up and down in unison. Having all strings play in unison creates greater density and thickness of sound as if to show just how strong the power of God is. The tenor sings in a high *tessitura* in most of the movement, reaching up to a high B-flat, the very top of a tenor's range. Listening to a tenor in such a high range often makes listeners sit on the edge of their seats, hoping that the tenor will make it! This kind of gesture is used often in opera. A tenor in his upper range ultimately signifies victory, leaving the audience almost breathless.

Movement IX: Esurientes implevit bonis (Solo for alto)

> *Esurientes implevit bonis, et divites dimisit inanes.*
> He has filled the hungry with good things, and sent the rich away empty.
> (Luke 1:53)

God fills the hungry ones who seek him with good things for both body and soul. In contrast, and for a third time in Mary's song, the ostensibly self-sufficient ones—this time the rich—are dealt with in the opposite way from which they expect: they are sent away empty. It is not wealth per se that is the problem, but the disposition of a human heart in relying on wealth rather than God for nourishment.

With a feeling of delightful contentment, the alto soloist and the recorders almost lovingly interpret this text. With a luxuriousness of sound, they seem to signify that the hungry are and will be filled with good things. The musical gesture of the first motif is that, in a single beat, there are two quick notes followed by a longer note—two sixteenth notes followed by an eighth note. A "stopping" quality at the end of this gesture seems to say, "I'm starting to feel full." While his method of motivic implication has been challenged, Albert Schweitzer refers to this figure as a "joy" motive. As the recorders continue their duet, they trade off which one has the long note and which one skips along; first one recorder plays a long note while the second dances in sixteenth notes, then they switch positions. Perhaps it is Bach's way of saying that all the hungry will have good things—first you, then me, but always both of us. The key is a happy F major, with the only harmonic movement to the dominant, a happy C major. Rather than initially speaking of the mighty or proud as in other movements, this time Bach changes to allow the lowly, the hungry to have first place. At the very end, Bach leaves the rich empty as the recorders abruptly stop, leaving just the bass line to play the last note. Powerfully symbolic!

Laud 4: Duet for solo soprano and bass

Virga Jesse floruit, Emmanuel noster apparuit.
From the root of Jesse, shall come our Emmanuel.
Induit carmen hominis, fit puer delectabilis.
In human form, as a delightful child.
Alleluia.

By the time of Bach, opera in the Baroque became the *musique du jour*. A composer's prestige was elevated if he wrote beautiful operas. As mentioned earlier, Leipzig's first choice to fill the post of cantor was one of the most prolific composers of all time, Georg Philip Telemann. He had written thirty-one operas, while Bach had written none. As such, the post in Leipzig would truly be a backward career step for Telemann. Many of Bach's melodies are perhaps his way of employing an operatic style, and *Virga Jesse floruit* is one of the pieces Bach wrote that comes close to being operatic.

The movement is completely filled with contrapuntal, long, florid melismas, which are traded back and forth between the soprano and the bass. Bach characterizes certain words and phrases as more important than others. In the text, *Emmanuel noster apparuit* (shall come our Emmanuel), *carnem hominis* (in human form), and *puer* (boy) are all treated with straight eighth notes for emphasis. Putting those words together, the meaning is: "a boy, who is our Emmanuel, shall come in human form." While each of the words begins a new contrapuntal section, they are not treated in a florid fashion. Bach declares the important text and then allows the duet to sing long melismas, suggesting the idea that we sing and rejoice in this important text, almost like extended bird songs.

Movement X: Suscepit Israel (Trio for solo soprano 1, soprano 2, and tenor)

Suscepit Israel puerum suum, recordatus misericordiae suae,
He has helped his servant Israel, in remembrance of his mercy,
(Luke 1:54)

In this verse, Mary returns to the beginning, to the greatest work of God: the Incarnation of the Son of God through whom there is salvation from sin, death, and hell. This, specifically, is the help of which Mary sings. The "remembrance of God's mercy" connects to the promise that God made to Abraham, which is addressed in the next verse.

The final solo movement, as suggested earlier, completes the succession of the solo movements, with one voice in several movements at the beginning, two voices in Movement VI, and finally a trio in Movement X. Bach was always very aware of the importance of the Trinity. The relationship of these three solo movements probably denotes another Trinitarian connection. This threesome can be frequently found in Bach's oeuvre (the lifework of a composer). In the rather gentle, but somewhat sad, key of G minor, this short movement is probably one of the most serious—almost painfully so. There is nothing florid or melismatic with the movement. Because the tempo is rather slow, although still contrapuntal, the moving eighth notes almost seem like wailing. Most of the moving notes are in a downward motion signifying the "lowly." And he has shown Israel mercy by sending his only Son. The movement also includes a beautiful, almost ethereal melody. The solo oboe plays one long note per bar, which soars high above the voices. God from on high has sent mercy to the Israelites. The line is a plainsong melody called *tonus peregrinus* (reciting tone) and has been traditionally associated with the Magnificat in the Lutheran church for years. For centuries the use of a *cantus firmus* (fixed melody), of which the *tonus peregrinus* is an example, was used as a kind of "ground bass" around which the other voices weave.

Movement XI: Sicut locutus est (Chorus)

sicut locutus est ad patres nostros, Abraham et semini eius in saecula.
as he promised to our forefathers, to Abraham and to his seed forever.(Luke 1:55)

God has not helped Israel on account of Israel's merit, but because of God's promise to Abraham, an act of pure grace. Through Abraham's natural seed, God promised to bless all the families of the earth. Mary, a daughter of Abraham, was the person through whom God chose for the blessing of bearing his Son. This is the foundation of the entire Gospel message.

Sicut locutus est (as he promised) brings to the listener an exciting, solid fugue in an old-fashioned a cappella style. Bach is recalling his predecessors in Leipzig, especially Johann Kuhnau, who filled the Leipzig post just before Bach. This style of composition had been around for a couple of centuries and was considered one of the most distinguishing styles for learned composers. The fugue starts with the foundation of all harmony, the bass line. The other voices are added in pitch order. Once again, the rising quality of the fugue subject recalls the work of Bach's compositional forebears and ascends toward God in heaven. But also, the addition of voices in pitch order seems to denote one generation after another. It culminates in the final five bars, sung by all in a unison rhythm using the words "to Abraham and his seed forever." The fugue is exciting, but holds back some of the excitement because of what is to come!

Movement XII: Gloria Patri (Chorus)

Gloria Patri, gloria Filio, gloria et Spiritui Sancto, sicut erat in principio, et nunc, et semper in saecula saeculorum. Amen.
Glory to the Father, glory to the Son, and glory to the Holy Spirit. As it was in the beginning, is now, and ever shall be, world without end. Amen.

Again, trumpets! The *Gloria Patri* has symbolized the end of the Vespers service for many, many years and still is used today. It invokes excitement, but also a release from the many emotions felt in the worship service before the *Gloria Patri* arrives. The *Gloria Patri* is in two parts. In the first part, the words are *Gloria Patri, gloria Filio, gloria Spiritui Sancto*. It could not be more indicative of Bach's foundation for his work and life because of the Trinitarian triplets and the three-part opening of the movement. Once again, trumpets are in a threesome! Punctuating the word *gloria* each time, the trumpets add that stentorian (i.e, extremely loud), regal character of an important event. The movement is grand and the tempo is slow and deliberate, denoting the importance of this section of the text. Like the *sicut locutus est* (as he promised), the addition of voices from the bass up says "yes," Abraham's seed will last forever and is for all generations.

The second part is like a musical pun. With *sicut erat in principio* (as it was in the beginning) Bach beautifully ties the *Magnificat* together by recalling the motives found in the very beginning of his *Magnificat*. It is both clever and playful. The very beginning had a long florid instrumental introduction before the actual choral entrance, but this time there are only two bars in the instrumental introduction to the voices. Bach says, "Now the piece is complete, a unified whole." Mary's magnifying God lasts into eternity.

THE TRANSPOSITION FROM E-FLAT MAJOR TO D MAJOR (BWV 243)

The final chapter of Bach's *Magnificat* is its transposition to D major (BWV 243) in 1733 for the Feast of Visitation. The one in E-flat included the Lauds, whereas the version in D includes none of the Lauds. When the Lauds are included, the piece is specifically for the Christmas season. But the actual Vespers service is a service for the entire church year. Eliminating the Lauds allows the *Magnificat* to be used all year long. Another change in the D major version includes the use of transverse flutes, a more modern version of the flute, replacing the recorders. Also, for the baroque trumpets a piece in the key of D is much easier to play than a piece in E-flat. With these changes, Bach's *Magnificat* truly has become a piece for all seasons.

5

Luther and Lutheranism on Mary in an Ecumenical Context

Mariology in the Orthodox and Roman Catholic traditions, constituting two-thirds of Christendom, is a challenge that has to be answered by every new generation of children of the Reformation.

—Heiko Oberman[1]

These words about Mariology, the area of theological inquiry focusing on the Mother of Jesus, were spoken by Reformation scholar Heiko Oberman in 1964, but they are as applicable today as they were over fifty years ago. Whereas today the Roman Catholic and Eastern Orthodox Churches comprise less than two-thirds of worldwide Christianity, taken together they are the still the largest as well as the oldest Christian denominations, which is why we consider them here. In contrast, Lutherans comprise less than 5 percent of worldwide Christianity. Oberman's challenge for us today is to clearly articulate Martin Luther's views of Mary and that of the Lutheran Church by comparing and contrasting these views with those of the Roman Catholic and Eastern Orthodox Churches. In this comparison and contrast, the core issues for Lutherans have to do with the

---

1. Oberman, "Virgin Mary in Evangelical Perspective."

relationship of Scripture to tradition when defining Christian truth in light of the doctrine of justification by faith alone.

With respect to defining Christian beliefs, Roman Catholicism holds to both Scripture and tradition as sources of truth. But the pope always has the final say as to what is authoritative tradition, which led Pope Pius IX to say, on July 16, 1870, "I am the tradition." For Eastern Orthodoxy, Scripture is one category among a number of categories making up a unified, authoritative Tradition of Christian truth. As Orthodox Bishop Kallistos Ware has written: "Such are the primary elements which from an outward point of view make up the Tradition of the Orthodox Church—Scripture, Councils, Fathers, Liturgy, Canons, Icons. These things are not to be separated and contrasted, for it is the same Holy Spirit which speaks through them all, and together they make up a single whole, each part being understood in the light of the rest."[2]

In contrast, Luther and Lutheranism came to hold two principles from which church tradition must be evaluated. The first principle, which has been called the "formal principle" of the Reformation, is *Scripture alone,* which denies that tradition per se can be authoritative. The second principle, which has been called the "material principle" of the Reformation, is *justification by faith alone,* apart from good works. Justification by faith alone excludes any tradition that attempts to combine good works with faith as necessary for salvation. But these two principles do not operate separately from each other. They are to be taken together, as theologian Oswald Bayer has rightly stated:

> Both [*Scripture alone* and *justification by faith alone*] are one and the same: wrapped up in the event that takes place when the righteousness of God is actually given as a gift, at the moment the *promisso* [i.e., the proclamation of the Gospel] is articulated . . .[3]

Thus, in the proclamation of the Gospel, these two principles work together as one. They can be distinguished for the sake of theological clarity, but not separated. With this foundation, we turn to specific areas of belief about Mary among these Christian churches.

---

2. Ware, *Orthodox Church*, 206.
3. Bayer, *Martin Luther's Theology*, 75–76.

THE BIBLE AND THE CREEDS: JESUS WAS BORN OF THE VIRGIN MARY

The Roman Catholic, Orthodox, and Lutheran churches all subscribe to the belief in Jesus' miraculous birth as the biblical birth narratives testify: Jesus was conceived by the Holy Spirit and born of the Virgin Mary. These three churches also subscribe to the Nicene Creed. In addition to the Nicene Creed, the Roman Catholic Church and the Lutheran Church also subscribe to the Apostles' Creed and the Athanasian Creed, but neither the Roman Catholic Church nor the Lutheran Church makes much current use of the Athanasian Creed. The Orthodox Church does not subscribe to either the Apostles' Creed or the Athanasian Creed because neither of these were proclaimed at an ecumenical council of bishops and theologians in the early church. The Nicene Creed, however, was proclaimed at the ecumenical council held at Nicaea in 325. The Virgin Mary is named specifically in the Nicene Creed and the Apostles' Creed, but she is not mentioned by name in the Athanasian Creed.

One may wonder why the Lutheran Church accepts the creeds, since they are part of church tradition and not part of the Bible. How does this square with the Lutheran principle of *Scripture alone*? The answer is that Lutherans understand the creeds as a brief summary of scriptural truth. In regard to Jesus' birth, the Apostles' Creed reads, "I believe in Jesus Christ ... born of the virgin Mary,"[4] whereas the Nicene Creed reads, "We believe in one Lord, Jesus Christ. ... For us and for our salvation he came down from heaven; by the power of the Holy Spirit he became incarnate from the virgin Mary, and was made man."[5] Although worded differently, both proclaim the virgin birth, which Martin Luther always believed and taught. Although he was falsely accused of teaching that Mary was not a virgin when she gave birth to Jesus and that Joseph was Jesus' real father, he refuted the false charges in his 1523 treatise titled *That Jesus Christ Was Born a Jew*.[6]

---

4. Inter-Lutheran Commission on Worship, *Lutheran Book of Worship*, 85.
5. Ibid., 85.
6. *LW* 45:199.

Luther and Lutheranism on Mary in an Ecumenical Context

THE THIRD ECUMENICAL COUNCIL: MARY AS THEOTOKOS

The third ecumenical council, which was held at Ephesus in 431, made an important statement about the Virgin Mary: she was given the Greek title *Theotokos*, which means "God-bearer" or "Mother of God." Once again, this faith claim about Mary is shared by the Roman Catholic Church, the Orthodox Church, and the Lutheran Church. In his *Commentary on the Magnificat*, Luther referred to Mary as the "Mother of God" twenty-five times, whereas he referred to the "Virgin Mary" only nine times. Clearly, the teaching that Mary is the Mother of God was very important to Luther, and is acknowledged as an important teaching by the Lutheran Church as well. Mary as the Mother of God is very much in keeping with the biblical witness to the Incarnation. Bishop Kallistos Ware of the Orthodox Church sums up the importance of connecting the *Theotokos* to the doctrine of the Incarnation (i.e., that God himself became flesh through Mary's giving birth to Jesus):

> When the Fathers of the Council of Ephesus (431) insisted on calling Mary *Theotokos*, it was not from any desire to glorify her on her own, but because only so could they safeguard the correct doctrine of the Incarnation. They were concerned not with some optional title of devotion, but with a dogma that lies at the very heart of the Christian faith: the essential unity of Christ's person. . . . What Mary bore was not just a man more or less closely linked to God, but a single and indivisible person who is God and man at once. "The Word was made flesh" (John 1:14): that is why Mary must be termed *Theotokos*. . . .[7]

Lutherans agree that Mary as *Theotokos* is directly connected to the scriptural witness of the Incarnation. Perhaps the most succinct and helpful statement of Mary as *Theotokos* is given by the theologian Jaroslav Pelikan: Mary is the "Human mother of [the] One who is God."[8] Even though Luther and Lutheranism agree on the *Theotokos*, Lutherans do not find much said about this truth in their churches today, perhaps because it might sound "too Catholic." The theologian Robert W. Jenson[9] gives the issue its utmost clarity:

---

7. Ware, "Mother of God in Orthodox Theology and Devotion," 170–71.
8. Pelikan, *Mary Through the Centuries*, 55.
9. No relation to Bradley Jenson.

> As for Mary's being *Theotokos, mater dei*, Mother of God, that of course is formal dogma for Catholics, Orthodox, and magisterial Protestants alike. . . . If one balks at *that*, one is simply a heretic.[10]

The *Theotokos* was integral to Martin Luther's understanding of Mary and Jesus, and it is long past time that the Lutheran Church recaptures this important ecumenical teaching that is so basic to understanding Mary and, more importantly, the doctrine of the Incarnation.

MARY AS THE QUEEN OF HEAVEN

Both the Roman Catholic Church and the Orthodox Church traditions ascribe to Mary the title "Queen of Heaven." That title for Mary has not been accepted by the Lutheran Church, although Martin Luther did not dispute the title as one that was appropriate for Mary.

However, Luther had two concerns about this title for Mary. First, he was concerned that the title can be easily misunderstood, as he made clear in his *Commentary on the Magnificat*:

> There should be limits to extolling her [Mary's] name, such as that of Queen of Heaven, even though it is true. Nevertheless, she is not a goddess and she cannot give aid or help, as the pious think when they pray to her and flee to her more than to God. She can give nothing, but only God can. . . .[11]

Second—and this is Luther's main point—God's choosing of Mary to be the mother of Jesus was "pure grace and not a reward."[12] Mary did not merit being chosen for this honor. No one could merit this honor, not even Mary. As Luther said, "worthiness for this kind of motherhood consisted in nothing else than that she was suited for it and appointed to it."[13] In no way did Luther want a notion of personal choice or merit to creep in to an understanding of Mary's calling to bear the Son of God. She was justified for that role by God's grace alone.

---

10. Jenson, "Space for God," 50.
11. See page 51.
12. See page 50.
13. See page 50.

Luther and Lutheranism on Mary in an Ecumenical Context

ON THE QUESTION OF MARY'S PERPETUAL VIRGINITY

The Roman Catholic and Orthodox churches hold to a doctrine of Mary's perpetual virginity; in other words, they believe she was a virgin her entire life. Thus, her marriage to Joseph was never sexually consummated. However, the Bible makes reference in Mark 6:3 to Jesus' brothers and sisters. How can that be if Mary and Joseph did not consummate their marriage? Roman Catholics and Orthodox Christians answer that question by holding that the Aramaic words for brother and sister also have a broader meaning as "kinsmen" or "cousins."

In fact, Martin Luther himself believed in Mary's perpetual virginity, but Luther was accused of denying this teaching and addressed the issue in the same treatise referenced earlier, *That Jesus Christ Was Born a Jew*. It is interesting to watch Luther deal with this question on the basis of *Scripture alone*:

> Scripture does not quibble or speak about the virginity of Mary after the birth of Christ, a matter about which the hypocrites are greatly concerned, as if it were something of the utmost importance on which our whole salvation depended.[14]

Luther says quite plainly that Scripture does not address the question of Mary's perpetual virginity, but he goes on to side with tradition, saying, "Actually, we should be satisfied simply to hold that she remained a virgin after the birth of Christ because Scripture does not state or indicate that she lost her virginity."[15] Again, Luther wrote this in his 1523 treatise *That Jesus Christ Was Born a Jew*. Did he ever change his position on this question? No. When Luther wrote the Smalcald Articles in 1537, he continued to refer to the "always virgin" Mary.[16]

Despite this reference, the Lutheran Church has subsequently treated this question as a matter of theological opinion about which Christians can disagree. As Luther himself suggests, belief in Mary's perpetual virginity (1) cannot be definitively determined on the basis of Scripture, and (2) has no bearing on the issue of salvation. Therefore, Luther's personal opinion in favor of belief in Mary's perpetual virginity is not binding on Lutherans.

---

14. *LW* 45:205–206.
15. Ibid., 206.
16. Kolb and Wengert, eds., *The Book of Concord*, 300.

ON THE ROMAN CATHOLIC DOCTRINES OF THE IMMACULATE CONCEPTION AND THE ASSUMPTION OF MARY

The doctrine of the Immaculate Conception developed through the tradition of the church but was given its final doctrinal form by Pope Pius IX in 1854. The dogma holds that the Virgin Mary was preserved from the stain of original sin at the moment of her own conception. It is summarized as follows:

> By the authority of Jesus Christ our Lord, of the Blessed Apostles Peter and Paul, and by our own: We declare, pronounce, and define that the doctrine which holds that the most Blessed Virgin Mary, in the first instance of her conception, by a singular grace and privilege granted by Almighty God, in view of the merits of Jesus Christ, the Savior of the human race, was preserved free from all stain of original sin, is a doctrine revealed by God and therefore to be believed firmly and constantly by all the faithful.[17]

However, the Orthodox Church does not hold to the formulation of the doctrine as defined by the pope because it implies that Mary was free from "all stain of original sin," which the Orthodox deny. The Orthodox generally object to the doctrine because, as Bishop Kallistos Ware writes, "It seems to separate Mary from the rest of the descendants of Adam, putting her in a completely different class from all the other righteous men and women of the Old Testament. From the Orthodox point of view, however, the whole question belongs to the realm of theological opinion. . . ."[18]

The traditional belief of Mary's Immaculate Conception was very much present in Martin Luther's time, although not in the final form given much later by Pope Pious IX. Luther considered the tradition a pleasing thought. Luther, following Augustine, "told his congregation that Mary had been conceived in sin but had been purified by the infusion of her soul after conception. Her purification was complete due to a special intervention by the Holy Spirit, who preserved her from the taint of original sin in anticipation of the birth of Christ."[19] At the same time, Luther held that the

---

17. The Immaculate Conception (*Ineffabilis Deus*), *Papal Encyclicals Online*.

18. Ware, *The Orthodox Church*, 259-260.

19. Eric W. Gritch, "The Views of Luther and Lutheranism on the Veneration of Mary," 238.

Luther and Lutheranism on Mary in an Ecumenical Context

traditional belief in Mary's immaculate conception should not become an official church teaching.

Lutherans did, in fact, reject the papal doctrine of the Immaculate Conception as it was formulated in 1854 primarily on the basis of the *Scripture alone* principle. In short, there simply is no scriptural basis for this doctrine. The fact that the pope's decree attempted to bind the conscience of Christians to a doctrine that has no scriptural basis lifted the issue out of the realm of theological opinion, where the Orthodox left the issue. As a result, Lutherans forthrightly rejected the doctrine.

The doctrine of the Assumption of Mary also developed through the medieval tradition of the church, and it was given its final doctrinal form much later by Pope Pius XII in 1950:

> By the authority of Jesus Christ our Lord, of the Blessed Apostles Peter and Paul, and by our own authority, we pronounce, declare, define it to be a divinely revealed dogma: that the Immaculate Mother of God, the ever Virgin Mary, having completed the course of her earthly life, was assumed body and soul into heavenly glory.[20]

The Orthodox Church also accepts the doctrine of the Assumption of Mary as a part of its unified Tradition, but not on the authority of the pope. As with the doctrine of the Immaculate Conception, Martin Luther affirmed traditional belief in Mary's assumption. Here again, Luther's personal belief in the assumption of Mary is not binding on Lutherans. The Lutheran Church, on the basis of the *Scripture alone* principle, rejected this Roman Catholic doctrine, again due to its having no scriptural basis.

ON THE ISSUE OF INVOKING MARY AND OTHER SAINTS IN PRAYER

Both the Roman Catholic and Orthodox churches invoke Mary and the saints (as designated by church tradition) during prayer, but neither church seeks to *worship* Mary and the saints as they do God. For the Orthodox, invocation of the saints is often expressed through the use of icons (i.e., religious paintings) of particular saints in public worship and in private prayer.

---

20. Defining the Dogma of the Assumption (*Munificentissimus Deus*), *Papal Encyclicals Online*.

The Lutheran Church does not follow Roman Catholic or Orthodox church tradition in its understanding of what it means to be a saint. For Lutherans, sainthood is not a status reserved for a few exceptional Christians in church history. Rather, all Christians are justified by faith alone in Christ and are considered simultaneously and completely both saints and sinners. That being said, Lutherans do have an appreciation of many of the saints designated as such by Roman Catholic and Orthodox Church tradition as examples for living the Christian life. Nevertheless, Lutherans do not find any scriptural basis for invoking Mary and the saints in prayer. As can be seen in the liturgy for Holy Communion, Lutherans affirm that the saints in heaven join in the praise of God, but again, Lutherans stop short of invoking the saints in heaven because there is no scriptural promise that the saints in heaven are aware of or can respond to human invocations. Furthermore, in addition to the *Scripture alone* principle, the doctrine of justification is vital for Lutherans in settling the question of invoking saints in prayer, as is made clear by the following statement in volume VIII of the series Lutherans and Catholics in Dialogue, published in 1992:

> Lutheran[s] appeal to the doctrine of justification as the norm by which the practice of invoking the saints and Mary needs to be judged. Lutherans continue to ask why it is useful, or indeed necessary, to place one's trust not only in Christ but in the saints and in Mary as well. Justifying faith rests on the sufficiency of Christ, who alone is to be trusted as the Mediator through whom God, in the Holy Spirit, pours out the gracious gift of salvation.[21]

As for Martin Luther, his views on Mary and the invocation of the saints evolved over time. Theologian Eric W. Gritch wrote about the young Luther who was raised on the belief in the invocation of the saints:

> It is not surprising that [Luther as a] twenty-year-old law student cried out, "Mary, help!" when, on his way from Erfurt to Mansfeld in 1503, he fell and cut an artery in his leg with his dagger. Two years later, when frightened by a storm, he again cried out, "Help me, St. Anna! I will become a monk!"[22]

In his *Commentary on the Magnificat*, Luther briefly addressed the issue of the invocation of Mary and the other saints. Here is where we see Luther's

---

21. *The One Mediator, the Saints, and Mary: Lutherans and Catholics in Dialogue VIII.*, 37.

22. Eric W. Gritch, "The Views of Luther and Lutheranism on the Veneration of Mary," 235.

Luther and Lutheranism on Mary in an Ecumenical Context

views evolving. Luther wrote, "We ought to call upon [Mary] so that God will give and do what we ask for her sake. We should call on all of the other saints in the same way, so that the work remains totally God's alone."[23] He also said, "She does nothing; God does all."[24] Just so, the other saints do nothing; God does all. This stands in contrast to the earlier story mentioned above when Luther was frightened by lightening and appealed to St. Anne, believing that she herself could help him. In contrast, in Luther's *Commentary on the Magnificat* the saints do nothing; God does it all. But Luther had not yet jettisoned the tradition of invoking the saints. At the very end of Luther's *Commentary*, he still appealed for Mary to intercede on behalf of believers.

Luther's views on intercession continued to change, as we see in the publication of his *Personal Prayer Book* in the next year, 1522. Luther gave the Hail Mary an evangelical reworking that excluded the invocation of Mary: "We should make the Hail Mary neither a prayer nor an invocation."[25] How, then, is the Hail Mary to be understood? He wrote, "First, we can use the Hail Mary as a meditation in which we recite what grace God has given her. Second, we should add a wish that everyone may know and respect her [as one blessed by God]."[26]

By the time Luther wrote the Smalcald Articles (1537), he had moved to a complete rejection of the invocation of the saints in favor of invoking Christ alone:

> The invocation of the saints is also one of the abuses of the Antichrist that is in conflict with the first, chief article [regarding the divine majesty] and that destroys the knowledge of Christ. It is neither commanded nor recommended, has no precedent in the Scripture, and—even if it were a precious possession, which it is not—we have everything a thousand times better in Christ.[27]

Continuing in his rejection of the invocation of the saints in the Smalcald Articles, Luther does allow that "the angels in heaven pray for us"[28] and that the saints in heaven "perhaps" pray for us. But, "it does not follow from this that we ought to invoke angels and saints; pray to them. . . and consider

---

23. See page 51–52.
24. See page 51.
25. *Luther's Works*, vol. 43, 39.
26. Ibid., 39–40.
27. Kolb and Wengert, eds., *Book of Concord*, 305.
28. Ibid.

them as helpers in time of need...."[29] Luther continues, "As a Christian and saint on earth, you can pray for me, not only in one kind of need but in all necessities. However, on account of that, I ought not pray to you, invoke you, hold a festival, keep a fast, make a sacrifice, perform a Mass in your honor, and put my faith in you for salvation."[30] Such honor, Luther wrote, "belongs to God alone."[31]

In one particular respect, the contemporary ecumenical conversation regarding the invocation of saints would likely not be as problematic for Luther as it was in the sixteenth century. Luther's issue, as can be seen above, is that the practice of invoking the saints took the focus away from Christ by encouraging Christians to (1) seek help from the saints rather than Christ, (2) put faith in, and seek salvation from, saints rather than Christ, and (3) give honor to the saints rather than to God alone. However, current teachings of Roman Catholic and Orthodox Churches on the invocation of the saints take a different path from that to which Luther referred in the sixteenth-century Smalcald Articles.

This can be seen in the contemporary ecumenical dialogue in the United States between Lutherans and Catholics. Roman Catholics make it clear that for them, "Prayer to God and invocation of the saints do not stand in a competitive relationship, but in turning to the saints as intercessors one places trust ultimately in God and in Christ to whom all prayer is ultimately directed. No benefits are conferred by the saints that are not conferred by Christ himself."[32] Thus, for Roman Catholics, in the invocation of the saints, the saints are not the source of help; God is. The saints are not the source of salvation; God is. For Roman Catholics, the role of the saints in the process of invoking them is for the saints to pray to God for help on behalf of Christians alive on earth who request it. It is much like Christians who ask other Christians to pray for them or who request prayers from a congregational prayer chain: "[Roman Catholics] argue that the invocation of the saints, although not specifically commanded in Scripture, is not forbidden and seems to be a legitimate extension of the biblically approved practice of asking for the intercession of those living on earth (e.g., Rom 15:30–32; 2 Cor 1:11; Col 4:3)...."[33]

29. Ibid., 305.
30. Ibid., 306.
31. Ibid., 306.
32. Anderson et al., eds., *One Mediator, the Saints, and Mary*, 53.
33. Ibid., 52.

Likewise, from the Orthodox perspective, Bishop Kallistos Ware wrote:

> The Church is a single family, including both the living and the dead. It is an all-embracing unity in Christ, a unity expressed and realized above all through prayer. Here on earth it is our custom to pray for each other and to ask for one another's prayers: and this mutual intercession is an essential characteristic of our Church membership. To the Christian believer death is no final barrier, and so the bond of mutual intercession extends beyond the grave. We pray, therefore, for the faithful departed as well as for the living, and we ask the faithful departed in their turn to pray for us—not knowing exactly how such prayers prove effective, yet confident that in the sight of God's mercy no prayer offered in faith can ever be wasted. And among all the faithful departed for whose prayers we ask, to whom should we turn more frequently than to the Holy Virgin? If she is a model of what it means to belong to the Church, then she must be, among other things, a model of intercessory prayer.[34]

Luther was certainly in agreement about encouraging intercessory prayer among the saints on earth, as he stated in his *Commentary on the Magnificat*, "When you allow other people to intercede for you, that is right and proper, because we should pray for one another and help each other."[35] And, engaging in a bit of historical conjecture, it is unlikely that what was written above regarding contemporary Roman Catholic and Orthodox understandings of the invocation of the saints would have provoked the same sharp rejection of the practice that we read about in the Smalcald Articles written by Luther and quoted above. That being said, from the perspective of *Scripture alone*, it is unlikely that Luther would encourage the practice of the invocation of the saints in heaven. Therefore, from Luther's perspective and that of the Lutheran Church regarding prayer, it is right and proper for Christians to pray directly to God—but not invoke the saints in heaven—and it is acceptable to seek intercessory prayers from the saints on earth individually, from congregational prayer chains, and from prayers spoken during public worship.

---

34. Ware, "Mother of God in Orthodox Theology and Devotion," 174.
35. See page 43.

SUMMARY

As has been demonstrated in this chapter, Martin Luther's views of Mary evolved over time. From his youth, Luther was steeped in the veneration of Mary, but Luther reworked much of the churchly tradition about Mary to conform to the Reformation's *Scripture alone* and *justification by faith alone* principles. Nonetheless, he held to some non-scriptural beliefs about Mary, including her perpetual virginity, her immaculate conception, and her assumption into heaven. In these instances, Luther's views conformed more with Roman Catholic and Orthodox teaching than that of the Lutheran Church. However, Luther's personal views of these non-scriptural traditions about Mary were not and are not binding on the Lutheran Church. Furthermore, although this point is historical conjecture, it is reasonable to assume that Luther would have rejected the doctrines of the Immaculate Conception and Mary's Assumption when they were set in the form of a papal decree, as they were in 1854 and 1950, respectively. Ultimately, Luther did come to reject the non-scriptural tradition of the invocation of Mary and the saints, a tradition that continues to be shared by the Roman Catholic and Orthodox Churches.

From an ecumenical perspective, what is most important about Mariology is that the Roman Catholic, Orthodox, and Lutheran churches all share the biblical and creedal belief that Jesus was born of the Virgin Mary. These three churches also share belief in the important biblically-based declaration about Mary made at the third ecumenical council at Ephesus in 431: Mary is the Mother of God.

Appendix

Using This Book in a Group Setting

THIS BOOK CAN BE used individually or in a group setting. Several groups in Duluth, Minnesota, have used a prototype of this book together with recordings of Bach's *Magnificat*. The preface provides a list of recordings of Bach's *Magnificat* suitable for use with this book.[1] For a true Advent study, a group may wish to skip the Christmas Lauds present in Bach's E-flat major composition or simply use one of the many recordings in D major that do not include the Christmas Lauds. The suggested schedule for the study is three sessions of two hours each. Using that schedule, the material can best be covered with the timeline of activities listed below.

When working through each verse of the Magnificat and Bach's corresponding movement in his cantata, it is most helpful to begin by discussing Luther's comments on the corresponding verse in his *Commentary on the Magnificat* in chapter 3. Next, go through the explanation of the corresponding movement in Bach's *Magnificat* in chapter 4. (For convenience, chapter 4 provides a summary of Luther's comments prior to the explanation of each movement.) Finally, listen to a recording of the movement.

READINGS FOR SESSION 1

Foreword

Preface

---

1 The video-audio recording of Bach's *Magnificat* which is available on DVD requires the publisher's permission (i.e., EuroArts) for group use. There is no such requirement for any of the audio recordings on CDs.

Appendix

Chapter 1: Introduction to Luther's *Commentary on the Magnificat*

Chapter 2: Introduction to Bach's *Magnificat*

Chapter 3: Luther's introductory Letter of Dedication to Prince John Frederick through Luther's comments on Luke 1:46–48

Chapter 4: Bach's Journey to the *Magnificat* in E-Flat Major, and Movements I–IV

SESSION 1

- Discuss chapter 1
- Discuss chapter 2

- Discuss Luther's comments on Luke 1:46 in chapter 3
- Discuss Movement I of Bach's *Magnificat* in chapter 4
- Listen to a recording of Movement I

- Discuss Luther's comments on Luke 1:47 in chapter 3
- Discuss Movement II of Bach's *Magnificat* in chapter 4
- Listen to a recording of Movement II

Optional: Discuss the explanation of Laud 1 in chapter 4 and listen to a recording of Laud 1

- Discuss Luther's comments on Luke 1:48 in chapter 3
- Discuss Movement III of Bach's *Magnificat* in chapter 4
- Listen to a recording of Movement III
- Discuss Movement IV of Bach's *Magnificat* in chapter 4
- Listen to a recording of Movement IV

Using This Book in a Group Setting

READINGS FOR SESSION 2

Chapter 5: Luther and Lutheranism on Mary in an Ecumenical Context

Chapter 3: Re-read Luther's comments on Luke 1:46–48 and read Luther's comments on Luke 1:49–52

Chapter 4: Movements V–VIII

SESSION 2

- Discuss chapter 5

- Discuss Luther's comments on Luke 1:49 in chapter 3
- Discuss Movement V of Bach's *Magnificat* in chapter 4
- Listen to a recording of Movement V

Optional: Discuss Laud 2 in chapter 4 and listen to Laud 2

- Discuss Luther's *Commentary on the Magnificat,* Verse 50 in Chapter 3
- Discuss Movement VI of Bach's *Magnificat* in Chapter 4
- Listen to a recording of Movement VI

- Discuss Luther's comments on Luke 1:51 in chapter 3
- Discuss Movement VII of Bach's *Magnificat* in chapter 4
- Listen to a recording of Movement VII

Optional: Discuss Laud 3 in chapter 4 and listen to Laud 3

- Discuss Luther's comments on Luke 1:52 in chapter 3
- Discuss Movement VIII of Bach's *Magnificat* in chapter 4
- Listen to a recording of Movement VIII

Appendix

READINGS FOR SESSION 3

Chapter 3: Re-read Luther's comments on Luke 1:49–52, read Luther's comments on Luke 1:53–55, re-read Luther's Letter of Dedication to Prince John Frederick, and read Luther's Epilogue to the Magnificat

Chapter 4: Movements IX–XII

SESSION 3

- Discuss Luther's comments on Luke 1:53 in chapter 3
- Discuss Movement IX of Bach's *Magnificat* in chapter 4
- Listen to a recording of Movement IX

Optional: Discuss Laud #4 in Chapter 4 and listen to Laud #4

- Discuss Luther's comments on Luke 1:54 in chapter 3
- Discuss Movement X of Bach's *Magnificat* in chapter 4
- Listen to a recording of Movement X

- Discuss Luther's Luther's comments on Luke 1:55 in chapter 3
- Discuss Movement XI of Bach's *Magnificat* in chapter 4
- Listen to a recording of Movement XI

- Discuss Movement XII of Bach's *Magnificat* in chapter 4
- Listen to a recording of Movement XII
- Review the Theological Introduction in chapter 1 regarding *Soli Deo gloria* (To God alone be the glory)

- Discuss Luther's Epilogue to the Magnificat and compare it with Luther's Letter of Dedication to Prince John Frederick, both in chapter 3

Conclusion: Listen to Bach's *Magnificat* in its entirety while reviewing chapter 4 on each of the movements

Bibliography

Anderson, H. George, J. Francis Stafford, and Joseph A. Burgess, editors. *The One Mediator, the Saints, and Mary*. Lutherans and Catholics in Dialogue 8. Minneapolis: Augsburg Fortress, 1992.
Bach, Johann Sebastian. *Leipziger Weihnachtskantaten: Cantates de Noël à Leipzig (Christmas Cantatas from Leipzig)*. Performed by the Collegium Vocale Gent, conducted by Philippe Herreweghe. Harmonia Mundi 901781/82. Compact disc. 2003.
———. *Magnificat*. Performed by the Monteverdi Choir and the English Baroque Soloists, conducted by John Eliot Gardiner. Philips 411458. Compact disc. 1985.
———. *Magnificat: A Bach Christmas*. Performed by the New London Consort, conducted by Philip Pickett. Decca 4529202. Compact disc. 1997.
Bainton, Roland. *Here I Stand: A Life of Martin Luther*. Nashville: Abingdon, 1980.
Bayer, Oswald. *Martin Luther's Theology: A Contemporary Interpretation*. Translated by Thomas H. Trapp. Grand Rapids: Eerdmans, 2008.
Brecht, Martin. *Martin Luther: His Road to Reformation 1483–1521*. Translated by James L. Schaaf. Minneapolis: Fortress, 1985.
CrossAlone District, Lutheran Congregations in Mission for Christ. *The Cross and the Crown: An Eight Session Course in Lutheran Basics*. Minneapolis: Kirk House, 2011.
"Defining the Dogma of the Assumption" (*Munificentissimus Deus*). Papal Encyclicals Online. Online: http://www.papalencyclicals.net/Pius12/P12MUNIF.HTM.
Descartes, René. *Les Passions de l'âme*. Translated by John Cottingham. Cambridge: Cambridge University Press, 2006.
Fischer, Hans Conrad. *Johann Sebastian Bach: His Life in Pictures and Documents*. Minneapolis: Fortress, 2005.
Forde, Gerhard O. *On Being a Theologian of the Cross*. Grand Rapids: Eerdmans, 1997.
Galli, Mark. "The Fifth Evangelist." *Christianity Today*, July 28, 2000. Online: http://www.christianitytoday.com/ct/2000/julyweb-only/52.0c.html.
Gardiner, John Eliot. *Music in a Castle of Heaven: A Portrait of Johann Sebastian Bach*. London: Allen Lane, 2014.
Gritch, Eric W. "The Views of Luther and Lutheranism on the Veneration of Mary." In *The One Mediator, the Saints, and Mary*, edited by H. George Anderson, J. Francis Stafford, and Joseph A. Burgess, 235–248. Lutherans and Catholics in Dialogue 8. Minneapolis: Augsburg Fortress, 1992.
"The Immaculate Conception" (*Ineffabilis Deus*). Papal Encyclicals Online. Online: http://www.papalencyclicals.net/Pius09/p9ineff.htm.

Bibliography

Inter-Lutheran Commission on Worship. *Lutheran Book of Worship*. Minneapolis: Augsburg, 1978.

Jenson, Robert W. "A Space for God." In *Mary: Mother of God*, edited by Carl E. Braaten and Robert W. Jenson, 49–57. Grand Rapids: Eerdmans, 2004.

Kittelson, James M. *Luther the Reformer: The Story of the Man and His Career*. Minneapolis: Augsburg, 1986.

Kolb, Robert, and Timothy J. Wengert, editors. *The Book of Concord*. Minneapolis: Fortress, 2000.

Koopman, Ton, conductor. *Bach and Kuhnau: Magnificat*. Performed by the Amsterdam Baroque Orchestra and Choir. Recorded live at St. Thomas's Church, Leipzig, May 24, 2003. EuroArts 2053419. DVD. 2003.

Leaver, Robin A. "Bach and Luther." *Bach: Journal of the Riemenschnedier Bach Institute* 9/3 (1978) 9–12, 25–32.

Listenius, Nicolaus. *Rudimenta Musicae*. Rhau, Germany, 1533.

Lloyd, Rebecca. "Bach: Luther's Musical Prophet?" *Current Musicology* 83 (Spring 2007) 5–32.

Luther, Martin. *Commentary on the Magnificat*. Translated by A. T. W. Steinhaeuser. Anniversary ed. Minneapolis: Augsburg, 1967.

———. *Luther's Works*, vol. 21. Edited by Jaroslav Pelikan, translated by Jaroslav Pelikan and A. T. W. Steinhaeuser. St. Louis: Concordia, 1956.

———. *Luther's Works*, vol. 43. Edited by Gustav K. Wiencke, translated by Martin H. Bertram et al. St. Louis: Concordia, 1968.

———. *Luther's Works*, vol. 45. Edited by Walther I. Brant, translated by Walther I. Brandt et al. St. Louis: Concordia, 1962.

———. *Luther's Works*, vol. 46. Edited by Robert C. Schultz, translated by Charles M. Jacobs. Philadelphia: Fortress, 1967.

Marshall, Robert Lewis. *The Music of Johann Sebastian Bach: The Sources, the Style, the Significance*. New York: Schirmer, 1989.

Mattheson, Johann. *Das neu-eröffnete Orchestre*. Hamburg: Schiller, 1713.

———. *Der Vollkommene Capellmeister, Das ist Gründliche Anzeige aller derjenigen Sachen, dieeiner wissen, können, und vollkommen inne haben muss, der einer Capelle mit Ehren und Nutzen vorstehen will*. Hamburg: Christian Herold, 1739.

Oberman, Heiko A. "The Virgin Mary in Evangelical Perspective." *Journal of Ecumenical Studies* 1 (1964) 271–98.

Pelikan, Jaroslav. *Mary Through the Centuries: Her Place in the History of Culture*. New Haven, CT: Yale University Press, 1996.

Sasse, Hermann. *We Confess Jesus Christ*. Translated by Norman Nagel. St. Louis: Concordia, 1984.

Schubart, Christian. *Ideen zu einer Aesthetik der Tonkunst*. Vienna, 1806.

Schweitzer, Albert. *J. S. Bach*, vol. 1. Translated by Ernest Newman. New York: Dover, 1966.

Tammen, Bruce. "Why Did Bach, a Lutheran, Compose a Mass?" Chicagochorale.org. February 22, 2011. Online: http://www.chicagochorale.org/why-did-bach-a-lutheran-compose-a-mass/.

Ware, Timothy (Kallistos, Bishop of Diokleia). "The Mother of God in Orthodox Theology and Devotion." In *Mary's Place in Christian Dialogue*, edited by Alberic Stacpoole, 169–81. Wilton, CT: Morehouse-Barlow, 1983.

———. *The Orthodox Church*. 2nd ed. London: Penguin, 1997.

About the Contributors

THE AUTHORS

Peter A. Hendrickson, DMA, is the director of choral activities at Augsburg College, where he directs the Augsburg Choir and the Masterworks Chorale of Augsburg. He is also the artistic director of the Augsburg College Advent Vespers Celebration, one of the largest holiday music events in the Twin Cities, with over ten thousand worshipers participating annually. In 2009 he directed the Masterworks Chorale of Augsburg in a performance of Bach's *Magnificat*. He received a Doctor of Musical Arts degree in harpsichord and conducting from the Manhattan School of Music, a Master of Arts in historical musicology from Columbia University, and a Bachelor of Arts in music from Augsburg College. He also received the Performer's Certificate from the Hochshule der Künste, West Berlin, Germany, where he studied early music, harpsichord, organ, and conducting.

Rev. Bradley C. Jenson is a Certified Financial Planner (CFP) and a Certified Investment Management Analyst (CIMA) in Duluth, Minnesota. He has been an ordained minister for over thirty years, serving in the parish ministry for over twenty years before making a transition to financial services. He received an MDiv from Luther Seminary and a BA in religion from St. Olaf College. He and his wife, Jill, are coauthors of *The Essential Bible: A Summary of the Major Stories*.

THE TRANSLATOR OF LUTHER'S COMMENTARY ON THE MAGNIFICAT

Randi H. Lundell, PhD, is a grants manager and department administrator in the University of Minnesota Medical School. She received both an MA

About the Contributors

and PhD in German literature and philosophy from Northwestern University (Evanston, IL) after having completed a BA in music and German education at Concordia College (Moorhead, MN). Dr. Lundell has translated a number of theological books from German to English: *On Creation: Religion and Science in Dialogue*, by Walter Klaiber; *The Political Dimension of Reconciliation: A Theological Analysis of Ways of Dealing with Guilt during the Transition to Democracy in South Africa and Germany*, by Ralf K. Wüstenberg; *The Calvin Handbook*, by Herman J. Selderhuis and Henry J. Brown; and *The Righteousness of Faith According to Luther*, by Hans J. Iwand.

THE WRITER OF THE FOREWORD

Hans H. Wiersma, PhD, is an associate professor of religion at Augsburg College. He received both an MDiv and PhD in church history from Luther Seminary after having completed a BA in communications/media studies at the University of California, San Diego. He has served as a parish pastor in the Netherlands as well as in California and in Minnesota. In 2016, Fortress Press is scheduled to publish Dr. Wiersma's coauthored second edition of James M. Kittelson's *Luther the Reformer: The Man and His Career* (1983).